Analytical study of corporation taxation in India

Author
Dr.BHAVNA H.PARMAR
M.A., M.Phil. Ph.D.

Analytical study of corporation taxation in India
By
Dr.BHAVNA H.PARMAR

ISBN NO.978-93-5426-201-2

Copyright Dr.BhavnaParmar

Publication
Dr.BHAVNA H.PARMAR
49, B/H, SorabajiCompound,
GandhinagarSoc,Junavadaj
Ahmedabad-13

First Edition: 2020-21

Printer
Dr.BhavnaH.Parmar
49, B/H, SorabajiCompound,
GandhinagarSoc,Junavadaj
Ahmedabad-13

Dedication

Father
Mother
Brother

Index

Chapter 1

Introduction

India is the only country adopting the federal monetary system. The main powers are   the central government and the state government. The central government is the main authority in the federal finance system and the state government is the secondary authority. However, the central government has given some powers to the state government. Tax structure is discussed extensively, including direct and indirect taxation. A corporation tax is a direct tax whose share of the burden lies on the shareholders of the company. Corporation tax is generally a tax levied on a company. Hence, opinions were presented by various economists regarding corporation tax so before discussing corporation tax, it is important to discuss how the company came to be.

When the Industrial Revolution began and the era of trade began, the first person-owned firms existed, in which one person was owned and operated. But as the industry grew, new forms of business were coming into existence. Partnerships from the firm to the proprietorship and the gradual emergence of numerous generations, and the form of a large risk-taking company.

Generally the definition of a company is given below:

"A company is an artificial entity existing by law."

As the business development progressed, the proportion of investment and risk increased greatly. Thus, the company came into existence in large quantities. The company is considered a legally valid form. In the structure of the company the shareholders of the company are the true owners of the company but the company is managed by the salary managers.Todaypresent age the form of corporate firm is considered very large.

Indian professionals were given proper training to run the sector in order to select the corporate sector. India has a rich tax structure, which is found between the state and the central government. The Central Government imposes taxes on the entire income (excluding agriculture), while the State Government levies customs duty, excise duty and service tax. Taxes on VAT, stamp duty, land revenue etc. are collected by the State Government. IN this chapter we will discuss the factors related to the emergence of the corporate sector and the issues it touches.

Policies before and after independence:

Proper taxation was needed to raise government funds during the British period in India. In other words, the government needed a certain outcome in order to manage its finances. After independence, the government's objective was to bring about a radical change in the tax structure and policy. Economic policy is considered to be an important component for maximum social welfare through which the focus is on economic-social policies to achieve maximum social achievement. Taxation became one of the key determinants of economic policy for redistribution of income.

The corporate sector originated in the medieval period during the 18th and 19th centuries. An economist named A.B. Levy discusses the nature of the corporate sector in his book "Private Corporations and Their Control."

The word 'corporation' is derived mainly from the Latin word 'corporer' and in Sanskrit it means 'to be born of the body. 'The prevalence of the corporate sector has increased at present as each generation in the corporate sector is of a vast nature and the exchange of their financial transactions is very important.

1.2 History of corporate sector in India:

1.2.1   The beginning of the 19th century:

In the early stages of a long development, the company was very modest in its economy the companies were first established by European merchants in Madras, Mumbai and Bengal in India. For example, in India in Bengal and Mumbai in 1899-1900, 86% of total investment was done on companies. But there is no doubt that the proportion of investment in the growth of a joint stock company has been uniform. But due to the strike, the growth of the companies was not accelerated during 1892-1900, but during these years the last ten years were considered as motivating for growth. However, in view of the figures of 1882, the number of companies increased by 90 percent in 1892 and the capital investment of the company was increased by 70 percent. During the next eight years, the number of companies increased by 40 percent and their investment increased by 30 percent. In eight years, the number of companies was largely increased in banking, mill, press and business groups, when the law of the company was passed in England in 1862 when the act of limited liability of the business organization proved to be fundamental. And it was newly popularized in England in the last decade of the 19th century but the idea of the Indian business community couldn't take hold. But business opportunities were powerful enough to meet this. In fact, during the years from 1882 to 1900, the number of companies was paid 835 and their total investment was Rs 19.22 crore. The new form of business organization was used by a few emperors, their friends and their relatives. There were also some barriers to starting new research in the corporate sector

1.2.2 Twenty century

There was a urgent need for growth in the 19th century, so in the 20th century, growth was started rapidly. The contribution of industrialization is seen in the progress of India. In the year 1909-10, the number of joint stock companies increased to 2216 and their total investment amounted to Rs 61.00 crore. A 65 per cent increase in the number of joint stock companies means that about 75 per cent of the money (as per the figure of 1900) was paid on capital. One of the outstanding features here is that not only was the rate of companies increasing but their growth was also increasing rapidly. Thus, it was clear that the corporate sector was moving forward, which a good thing was compared to before independence.

During World War I, the total number of companies in India was 2744 and their total investment amounted to Rs.77 crore. During the first 15 (less than 15) centuries, the number of companies increased by 100 percent. And the number of companies increased from 1340 to 2744 and investment from Rs 34.90

crore to Rs 77 crore. Second, a growing during the period 1900-15, there were over 70 investments. Number of companies (1882-1900) invested 120 percent more in 1914 than in 1900, mainly.

Then the indigenous movement spread rapidly and the companies were encouraged that the investment of the company was considered as a factor responsible for the imported goods. Demand for commodities in India, such as cotton, etc. and the partition of Bengal, created a national sentiment among the people against the import of foreign goods and foreign goods were opposed. During this time J.N. Tata, a prominent Indian steel industry and his son Dorabji Tata founded the iron ore industry. Moreover, the government decided to change its policy. Thus, the government insisted on purchasing goods within the state of their country as far as possible. The investment support needed to encourage new corporations in India was very important.

1.2.3　First World War and after

The investment in stock issued by companies was developed during the years of the United States during the war of 1914-18 and during the presidency of the war. But due to the liquidity, the number of companies declined. The total investment of the companies was Rs 77 crore in 1914 while it increased to Rs 99 crore in 1918.War was a stopping factor in the demand for goods produced in the country. During the last period of the war, the growth of the machinery was greatly reduced due to the import of machinery.

The new company's position in the corporate sector became more important in order to meet the demand of the masses for rapid industrialization, and after the war, it became easier for the country to supply foreign machinery. During the period between 1918 and 1922, the number of joint stock companies increased by 5189 and its total investment increased by Rs 231 crore. In almost 8 years, when the number of companies increased twice, their investment had tripled. Nevertheless, satisfactory progress was made in 1922-32 during the next 10 years of progress in comparison. After 1923, the discrimination policy in favor of the pursuers of Indian goods had come into being. By contrast, total investment during the year 1914-22 was tripled (from Rs 77 crore to Rs231 crore).During the decade ending March 1932, during the growth of the companies, the shares of the companies were paid Rs. 55 crore. The number of companies increased from 5189 in 1922 to 7997 in 1932.After the global recession, the position of new companies in the corporate sector was changing.

Again, from 1932, the start of steady capital was started in companies. The number of companies increased from 7997 in 1932 to 11229 in 1937 and the investment paid to them increased from Rs.286 crore to Rs312 crore. Thus, during the 15 years i.e. 1922-1937, the number of companies increased substantially, from 5189 to 11229.The number of companies was doubled. In fact, the investment of companies increased from just Rs231 to Rs312 crore. In other words, the increase was about a third. During this period, the number of companies increased and investment also increased. Funds were raised by the new entrepreneurs to set up the company. In the corporate sector, competition was also on the rise.

India was separated from Burma in 1937 and as a result the number of companies and their investments declined by Rs 278 crore and Rs 25.7 crore respectively. Looking at the previous data, it appears that the number of companies is 2.6 percent but 8.2 percent investment. Several close companies had joined the Burma country, which caused a huge blow to the Indian economy. After being released from

Burma and two years after World War I, India had a total of 11114 companies and their investment was Rs 2,904 crore, but after being released from Burma, the reimbursement could not be completed.

During the war period, the number of companies increased but investment was disappointing. Of course, the economic situation in the world during the time of the interwar period, especially in the third decade, was in flux. During the recession years, India suffered losses as India manufactured primary commodities. The political environment is another factor in the slow growth of the corporate sector in India. Indians were more interested in political development than in the economic development of the country. Between the two movements and the absence of the people, Gandhi's Satyagraha collapsed between AD.1920-22 and 1930-32.In industrialization, the capitalists put their self-interest first and did not contribute to the economic development of the country.

1.2.4   during World War II:

During the Second World War in India, economic momentum was very limited. Again, during the Second World War; economic development can be easily seen through the inspiration of the government. For example, when textiles worth Rs.1415 lakh were imported in AD.1938-39, more than 90 percent was seen in AD.1942-43.

That is why some essential commodities were produced in the country itself. Imports of primary commodities such as paper, match boxes, glass, leather and soap in the country declined. Thus, the joint stock company was given more and more joint leadership in industrialization. When Japan and Russia entered the war, India became an important source of supply to the East China in the global conflict. Besides, India had become essential for industrialization to its full potential. After the end of December, 1942, a contract of Rs. 455 crore was arranged under the orders of the State Department. Many industries, such as iron and steel, wool chemicals, etc., tried to work with maximum capacity to contribute to the war, but during the crisis period in India, import of machinery from abroad was impossible. Thus the machinery of protection in India could not be made available.

1.2.5   in the post-war period:

When the war ended in 1945, there was an increase in the number of companies after the first year's war in an unprecedented joint construction to advance industrialization. In the country of India, the interest of the citizens was observed to take the growth rate higher to satisfy the demand of the consumers. In order to meet specific needs, underdeveloped countries such as Asian, Indonesia, etc. were led by China, Iran, Arab countries as the economy of the underdeveloped countries was disrupted during the war. They had to face economic hardship so new industries were established to restore the economies of such countries. Thus, the number of companies and their investment in the market increased sharply after the war period.

The number of companies doubled in six years between 19.1947-48 and 1949-50 and set an impressive record in investing. A new investment of Rs 95 crore has been made for the gradual investment of new capital in the sector. The number of companies in August 1947 after the Companies Act of the Government of India was about 2000 and their total investment was Rs 18 crore, which was done for Pakistan. Twenty years ago in 1937, when the partition of Burma broke out, there was a big crackdown against Pakistan, But the comments regarding the company law and order were registered in Pakistan along with the administration and, nevertheless, there was no information about how many companies moved to India and how much capital was in India. Yet, even after the partition of the country, the number of companies in the corporate sector was very small. But in 1947 the number had increased to 21653.The number was 22675 in the first year after the partition. In addition, the number of companies increased from 800 to 2000 due to the separation of Pakistan. With the acquisition of independence in August 1947, joint stock companies Moved in terms of numbers and power. As mentioned earlier, it played a brief role in accelerating the economic development of the Korean War to encourage the development of companies immediately after the partition period.

Thus, after 1951, economic activity in India became more or less guiding. But in 1951, five-year plans were made by the government to take India towards economic development. At the time of the first scheme (1951-56), a total of 1520 companies were doing business and the investment paid to them was Rs 235 crore. As the corporate sector continued to grow, the number of companies increased and their investment increased.

1.2.6 Private and public corporations in their respective development

In the post-independence period the corporate sector was divided into two parts. The dominance of public and private companies, especially public and private companies, was even higher. However, during this time the number of public companies was decreasing. And their investment was increasing. In 1917, the total number of private companies in India was 207 and their investment was around Rs.5.8 crore. In 1956, the number of companies increased to 20000 and their investment increased to Rs 334 crore. An increase of about 100 companies and a 60-fold increase in investment took place in 40 years. Moreover, more than half of the investments made in many private companies were in public companies in 1955-56.Looking at the figures from 1951 and 1959, the number of public companies saw a decline of around 46 per cent when their investment increased by 54 per cent. When the number of private companies declined by 21 percent, their investment increased by 400 percent.

The rate of growth of private companies was difficult to understand and the rate of inertia of public companies was also difficult to understand. The first were strong law firms that were operating under the leadership of the administration And some public companies were kicked out of the corporate arena. Second, the important reason was that the Indian capital was raised in a shrinking environment. It could easily have been created for private companies' incentives. The necessary protection of capital has shown a business spirit for corporate sector entrepreneurs to raise funds through public affairs. The benefits of limited liability absorb the gradual cycle of ownership. It is said that the deep roots of democratization in India are in the business ventures but they did not see the organizational revolution. Average investment in India has led to the development of adequate investment and, with a sense of direction; quality investment was made by some entrepreneurs only.

1.2.7 New and old companies

The growth of the corporate sector in India was growing historically. However, the number of companies in India was increasing. From the last century, World War II continued to grow at a steady pace, but while the corporate sector remained dominant and unique. Yet it cannot be said that growth in the corporate sector has been satisfactory. The company that existed and their capital grew as well. Companies are well established and their steady profits can be earned by earning another profit. There is an urgent need for a conducive environment for investment. In new ventures, the risks make the capital shrink.

Not only this, there is a disparity between the authorized and the paying capital. This ratio was approximately 225: 1 and 400: 1, respectively, in 1955-56 and 1953-54.In eight years, it was sown that capital gains more liquidity when borrowing capital is brought in when new registrations are made. With the growing success in the current environment of industrialization, the corporate sector is evolving and moving forward. Statistics show that during the first five-year plan, when the investment of new companies was Rs.25000, the average corporate sector investment was Rs.3 lakh per company. There was a disparity between new and old companies

1.3 Scope of Study:

The study of corporation tax is considered to be incredibly wide and comprehensive. Corporation tax is not only a tax levied on the company's income, but also relates to the company's profit and loss, the company's pre-tax profit and post-tax profit, how much dividends are paid to the company's shareholders, etc.

Corporation tax is levied on the income of the company and is levied by the government. Usually a company is a legally existing artificial person. Hence dividends are paid to the shareholders of the company as per the norms of the company. As well as some amount is kept as a separate fund in the form of undistributed profits.

1.4 Objectives of Study:

1. The study of corporate tax provides information on what reforms should be in corporate tax.

2. Corporate tax statistics provide forecasts for future research as they come from an organization like the Government of India's Budget.

3. Corporate tax plays a very important part in analyzing statistics.

4. The study of corporate tax also makes it easy to know how much corporate income contributes to India's total tax revenue and how much revenue the government receives from the corporate sector.

5. This study compares the corporate tax of one country with another country and the amount of corporate income tax earned by one state within another country.

1.5 Methodology:

In this short research paper, visited the Gujarat Chamber of Commerce in person and got the information of corporation tax from there as well as secondary information has been used in the research.

Chapter 2

Literature review

Company taxation is a controversial tax in the tax structure. Economists disagree on whether to tax the first company. In general, according to experts, the tax on the company is considered as the tax on the shareholders. There is still disagreement as to whether the corporate tax deduction falls on the shareholders or on the consumer or wage earners. Inflation during World War II raised the question of the calculation of the depreciation fund. Accordingly, there was a controversy as to whether the depreciation fund should be considered at the original price of the machinery or machinery or purchased at the current price. Ultimately, there is disagreement over whether or not the company's total profits or dividends will be divided.

Most companies pay double tax on their income. One company pays tax before distributing dividends and the other in the form of dividends. When this income is received by the shareholders, their income is taxed. On the other hand, business income other than company is taxed only once. First of all, there is not much difference between the income of the company and the income of the shareholders. The company has a large number of shareholders in its revenue. As such, shareholders have no control over the company's revenue. While shareholders can share their income at any time, there is no difference between the income of private companies and shareholders.

The income of public companies and the income of shareholders are not considered the same, as shareholders can use their income independently while the income of a company cannot be considered as one because its shareholders cannot use it independently. Therefore, since the income of shareholders and the company is different, different taxes are levied on the income of both, so the question of double taxation does not arise. However, it becomes necessary to check whether the tax deduction of the company tax falls on the shareholders. The argument of double taxation becomes plausible if the taxation of the company tax falls only on the shareholders, but the study of company taxation does not show consistency among the various economists.

According to some economists, the tax on the company has been considered as a principle of profit. In his view, the company must be taxed on the benefits it receives from the states. When Companies are registered the state gives them some because the company is an artificial person that legally exists. The company carries out productive operations using its own name, as well as legally acquiring all other companies. By law the company acquires a living personality. In addition, the company benefits from the cost incurred by the state for training craftsmen, engineers and scientists. In underdeveloped or developing countries the company reaps the benefits of public services such as roads, transportation, electricity, education, health, etc. Not only that, business associations like individual ownership and partnership firms also benefit indirectly so they should also be taxed.

In the theory of profit, it is difficult to get the benefit of who has benefited from most of the activities that the company does. On the contrary, if the state benefits the company, then the company also benefits the society. In the management of the company, the company has the savings of many individuals, which can be used productively and through it many people can be employed. If special benefits are given to the company by the state, then the company should collect tax not on the basis of profit but on the basis of the profit received. Thus, taxation is justified by the principle of profit, but company taxation cannot be justified.

Like the principle of profit, company tax is also calculated on the basis of taxable power. Just as individuals are taxed according to their ability to pay taxes, so should companies be taxed according to their ability to pay taxes? The principle of the power to pay taxes applies to individuals or organizations, but not to the company. The principle of the power to pay taxes in company taxation goes against it.Nevertheless, the company tax structure is kept progressive But in reality the number of shareholders of a company making more profit may be less while the number of shareholders of a less profitable company may be more.

Yet it is often argued that the tax on the company is mostly the tax on the members of the company if a tax is levied on a company for any reason, this tax should be paid to the members of the company. Hence the tax levied in India was levied on the company. Taxes are levied and if they stunt the growth of companies, it can have an adverse effect on wealth creation and future employment. The tax on the company is levied on a certain percentage of the company's income. The progressive tax structure in India is sometimes not desirable for the company as the tax rate is kept the same for most companies. In the case of taxation, if the tax is levied only on the earnings received by the individuals, then the earnings of the corporation which are not paid as dividends are evaded from the current tax. Thus, the corporation is used in such a way that it can be reinvested without levying tax on profits. If the corporation is treated as an individual for tax purposes and the general personal income tax rates are applied to it, then the accepted principles of tax distribution are violated.

There are two different views on the corporation's income tax policy. It ignores the existence of corporation if considered for the purpose of a consolidation. Income tax is generally levied on the income received by an individual from a corporation in the same manner as in other enterprises. In corporations, the burden of taxation is mostly on individuals, so the principle of power of taxation is not observed. Another argument was made that and salaried managers. For many years the question was accepted that corporation income tax does not differ. As an individual firm, a tax with an equal percentage of net income will not affect the price of the product as the production surface continues to give the highest profit before and after. Even if all the figures are subtracted from a given percentage, the previous high is still high. Or in tax burden does not rely on business forms. This can be tax neutral. The opposite effects are therefore avoided. In addition the company has a legally separate entity. The company is Therefore managed by its shareholders other words, marginal income or marginal expenses are not affected by the tax and changes in prices or products are not beneficial.

According to the traditional argument, tax change is not possible in the long run. In the previous analysis, it was assumed that to the extent that the tax applies to net profit, it will not have any effect on the investment policies of older or newer generations as the required return factor is not taxed. Corporation income tax is therefore not only limited to net profit, but also special. The difference in income tax is argued in terms of business firms and the size of the investment. However, it is a conventional argument that firms cannot directly deflate income tax in full competition. This argument also applies to the absolute monopolist. But now there is neither full competition nor complete monopoly. But the feature of an oligopoly competition exists. The purpose of firms in oligopoly is to make maximum profit. According to Fellner, it is rare for firms to achieve this goal. If the corporation tax is levied or increased and the firms consider the tax a matter of expense, they will bring down the price. The same tax will be levied on all the firms in the industry which have the same price and all the firms will benefit till they reach the maximum level.If profits increase in such a way then why taxes do not increase because in a minority market monopoly one generation does not follow another generation.

If the policy of leadership is adopted, the possibility of tax evasion increases if the objective of reasonable or satisfactory profit is achieved. But on the other hand there are many difficulties in the path of complete diffraction. This is because one firm makes more profit through sales than the other. Hence the profit margins on each item vary from firm to firm. Thus firms are incapable of tax evasion. Thus a small tax evasion is almost inevitable in times of high demand. The effect of the tax on investment also plays an important role on the principle of non-tax evasion. To the extent that taxes do not differ quickly, it reduces net receipts from withheld capital. If the government has a large share of the profits, the corporation's management will not take any steps to expand. Doubling the dividend income reduces the attractiveness of the stock investment. As well as the purchase of fixed income securities and cash becomes more attractive in comparison, the flow of share capital decreases.

Thus, corporation income tax does not apply to the owner's capital gains but to net economic profits. It is quite possible that declining income from investment in the short term will create unemployment. But the rate of pre-tax receipts should be higher than the tax-free rate to sustain full employment in the long run. The period for diversification is very long in stable industries with high fixed investment characteristics but the size of investment in a dynamic economy is always increasing. And taxes help reduce the proportion of new investments. Therefore, the effect of tax on investment is felt soon.

Chapter 3

Corporation tax structure and amendments

(Pre and Post after 1991)

Structure of corporation tax in India and reforms in corporation tax before and after 1991.

1. Structure and rationality of corporation tax

2. Highlights of the Corporation Tax Reform

- 3.Polite versus integrated system

- 4.Rate structure

- 5.Revenue income

- 6.Tax incentives

- 7.The collapse of the tax base

1. Minimum alternative tax in India

Calculation of alternative tax

(1)   Structure and rationality of corporation tax:

Corporation tax is levied on the company's profits. In almost every country the important tax base is included in the composition of the company's revenue when it is exploited for the collection of revenue. Corporation taxes are considered reasonable for many reasons. The reasons are as follows:

1.   Corporate income provides an important tax base for the mobilization of resources for the country.

2.   Most companies have a monopoly position and make huge profits. A portion of the profits is collected by the state to cover public expenses. The corporation therefore acts as part of a tax on tax monopoly rent or net profit.

3.   If the company is not taxed, foreign owners who are not subject to personal income tax are completely exempt from paying taxes.

4.   The corporation takes advantage of the limited liability privilege that results in a huge amount of capital for investment as a result of the dynamics. By virtue of which the benefits provided to the companies are far removed from the benefits provided by the government.

5.   Some of the barriers to personal taxation are corporate income. If the tax is levied on the dividends earned by the shareholders, it is necessary to levy tax on the company's profits to eliminate the possibility that the profits reserved by the corporate will escape tax.

6.   Taxation of foreign capital income from the exploitation of international market power is desirable.

7.   When economic profits are not completely tax-free under the local system, foreign capital has to be taxed for both the country's capital exports and capital imports.

8.   In all instances the 'local exclusive rent' of multinational firms is taxed on such profits without affecting the investment.

In addition, the flow of modern economic activities flows through the corporation's pipeline. Ordinary corporate firms are simple and stable through their information and transactions. Political barriers to higher and direct taxation, based on the source, can be a good way for the progressive factors of corporate taxation. Economists argue that corporate taxation may not be desirable in many discrepancies and costs as a result of corporate taxation. Bird argues that the dark side of corporate tax analytics in the public economy literature is too small for economists to imitate for economists because there is so little purpose and comprehensiveness that significant economic benefits can be gained by eliminating and reducing corporate taxes. Conversely, prominent economists and proponents of corporate taxes say that corporations do not pay enough taxes for tax purposes.The government was therefore deemed worthy of public opinion to avoid any problem.

The history of corporation taxation in modern India dates back to 1860.Personal income tax came into existence this year and was levied accordingly. The basic tax on corporate income based on the British model is paid by shareholders or the tax paid by companies is deducted from the shareholders' own income tax liability or undistributed profits. This tax has been known as the super tax since 1940 and is now known as the corporation tax. Most of the shareholders could not get any credit in the super tax. Major changes were made to this tax in 1960-61.The corporation was treated as a legal entity for completely different tax purposes and for income to be paid on behalf of the shareholder as well as taxable by closed companies. Tax credit income to shareholders from income tax paid by companies was not considered valid. Under the new system, companies were liable to pay tax on undistributed profits and shareholders were again taxed on their dividends, which included total revenue. The calculation of what is thus considered a double tax has also been criticized by various economists. Instead of abolishing shareholder dividend tax in 1997-98, domestic companies now pay tax on shareholders' shared profits.

(2)   Matters of Corporation Tax Reforms:-

The main points of the Corporation Tax Reforms that were made before 1991 and after 1991 are as follows:

1.   Polite versus integrated system

2.   Rate Structure

3.   Revenue Income

4.   Tax Incentives

5.   The collapse of tax revenue

The contribution of corporation tax has been more important than the developed personal income tax. This complex system has undergone changes from time to time. Looking at revenue as well as equality as well as a conducive environment, it is seen that corporate tax reform was needed to increase domestic foreign investment. And the major areas related to it, such as the tax structure, the elongated special incentives, the erosion of the tax base, as well as the existence of a large number of zero tax companies, also needed to be improved.

(1)   Polite vs. Integrated system:-

An important improvement in corporate taxation was that the fully integrated system was more practical when the corporate structure was adopted in a decent manner. Income tax was levied independently under civilized corporate tax, as well as double taxation on the company's income and dividends to shareholders. In an integrated system, taxes should be levied according to the principle of taxation. Parts of the corporate sector are the tube through which the flow of income flows from the owners to the last individuals. Therefore, they should pay tax on corporate income which is in the hands of individuals.

The Direct Tax Task Force (2002) after deliberation on this system pays the minimum rate of personal income tax in the various two-way integrated type of system which is taxed at the corporate level and relieves shareholders from long-term capital gains. However, the task force (2002) argues that the integrated system only serves the purpose and that the accounting profit bears the full burden of corporate tax. As such, effective corporate tax liability is equivalent to a statutory corporate tax rate. This becomes possible if there is no divergence between the taxable base and the accounting profit for companies that usually arises due to various tax incentives and artificial deductions. The process towards implementation of the recommendations of the task force was introduced in the government.

(2)   Tax Structure:

So far, the corporate tax rate in India has been very high and the corporate tax structure is complex. Because very large companies (companies in which the public has a vested interest) and very small companies (companies in which the general public has no vested interest) as well as very small companies in very small rates As we can see, in the main body of 1960-61, non-domestic companies were classified in two ways.(1) Widely dominated companies and (2)Companies with narrow dominance. In 1984-85, the tax rates for broad-based companies and narrow-dominated companies were 57.75 per cent and 68.25 per cent, respectively. On-domestic companies were taxed at 73.5 per cent. Now the tax rates in domestic companies in 1991-92 were assessed as follows. Large-dominated companies were taxed at 40 per cent and narrow-dominated companies at 50 per cent on commercial or investment companies and other companies at 45 per cent. Similarly, the tax rate for foreign companies was 65 per cent in the same year. The year 1992-93 was mainly known as the assessment year. In the middle of this, domestic companies were influenced by the corporate income of the dominant companies, so their tax rate was 45 percent and the rate of corporate income tax paid by these companies, such as commercial companies or other companies, was 50 per cent, regardless of whether the entire narrow-dominated companies were considered. As well as in foreign companies the tax rate was applied 65 per cent. Thus, the first attempt by the government in the 1994-95 budgets was to revise the corporate income tax rate structure. It was also aimed at giving proper impetus to the corporate sector so as to create huge competitive power by increasing savings and investment. Structural objectives were initiated in 1991 to cultivate this consensus. In this context, efforts were made to bridge the gap between the vast majority of domestic companies and the narrow dominant ones. And the same rate was fixed at 40 per cent for all domestic companies. With it the rates of foreign companies were reduced to 55 per cent. But if there are domestic companies, a surcharge of 15 per cent was levied on additional taxable income. With this result, the effective rate for domestic companies (with surcharge) was 57.5 per cent in case of narrow-dominated companies and 51.75 per cent in case of large dominant companies. In the 1996-97 budgets, the surcharge was reduced from 15 per cent to 7.5 per cent. In the 1997-98 budgets, there was a reduction of 55 per cent to 48 per cent for non-domestic companies and 40 to 35 per cent for domestic companies. While in other countries current rates declined. But again in the budget for 1999-2000 a surcharge of 10 per cent was levied as a temporary measure of the additional equipment that became available.

(3) Revenue Income

In terms of revenue in the corporate sector, there were also significant changes. The contribution of corporate tax in general is even more important than personal income tax because some difficulties were also associated with the post-system time in a developing economy. The image of a corporation exists and generally forms an important tax base. Considering this issue, corporate tax revenue was not very satisfactory. However, its contribution is much higher than that of personal income tax. The following table shows the revenue income from corporation tax:

Table 1

Contribution of corporation tax to the total tax revenue of the Central Government

In crore rs.

Year	Revenue income by Corporate Tax (2)	Total Tax Revenue (3)	Percentage (2 +3)
1970-71	371	3207	11.56
1980-81	1311	13320	9.84
1990-91	5335	57513	9.27
1991-92	7853	68436	11.47
1992-93	8899	74566	11.93
1993-94	10060	75692	13.29
1994-95	13822	92295	14.97
1995-96	16487	111237	14.82
1996-97	18567	128762	14.41
1997-98	21360	142720	14.96
1998-99	27050	148700	18.19
1999-2000	30850	175860	17.44

Source: RBI, Currency and Finance Report, 1991-92 and 1993-4, Indian Government, Budget 1995-96 and 1999-2000.

The share of corporate tax in total taxes in the central government fell from 11.56 per cent in 1970-71 to 9.27 per cent in 1990-91.It has since grown steadily, reaching 18.19 per cent in 1998-99.But the revenue generated by the corporation tax increased .The country was entering a large corporate sector. But the revenue generated by the corporation tax increased .The country was entering a large corporate sector. But the revenue generated by the corporation tax increased .The country was entering a large corporate sector.

(4)   Tax Incentives:

Various concessions have been given for special incentives by investment such as tax holidays especially in corporate income tax. These facilities are provided for the importance and development of developing countries. These are developing countries that have been heavily criticized. The incentives that were given for investment caused some difficulties. This has been repeatedly pointed out. It was observed by the World Development Record (1988) that the incentives that are given for tax place more emphasis on tax instruments and this pressure comes from various purposes. The benefits of incentives encourage mixed consent and non-productive actions. If the amount of incentives is small, the economic benefits are limited and if the amount of incentives is large, the revenue remains special for the fall of the tax. The corporate tax base in India has collapsed because of the idea of excessive concessions and the idea of reducing tax incentives. Tax reform should have significantly reduced taxes on austerity and equality. It is imperative that all such incentives be kept away in the tax system except for the only important required tax. Various incentives were given by the government which is required for the minimum reduction which is given as follows:

(A)   Depreciation compensation:-

In most countries depreciation compensation is determined for incentives while the net profit of tax is considered as the tax base while the cost of machinery is deducted from the cost of depreciation to cover the cost of equipment houses. Migrated tools are found. In 1988-89, in a very complex system in India, depreciation compensation includes various compensations such as general compensation, initial compensation, additional compensation time or compensation for various taxes for general depreciation. The System Reforms Commission investigated the matter for necessary simplification and suggested that a consolidation of various returns as well as a normal rate of 331/3 per cent for machinery and plant should be maintained. Depreciation costs were calculated to calculate original costs or old costs. Hence the failure to redistribute these instruments at the time of inflation thus allowing higher returns.

The recommendations of the Economic System Reform Committee became more effective in the year 1988-89.According to this committee, various compensations were consolidated and hence the depreciation compensation was kept at 33 1/3 per cent. It was later reduced by 25 per cent in 1991-92.The Tax Reform Committee, which examines matters affecting or touching depreciation, therefore approves a 25 per cent depreciation compensation on a domestic company.

(B)   Other concessions

A variety of concessions are offered from time to time. The Development Exemption Act was introduced in 1955 but did not last long. Exemption for development was introduced in 1985.Under this Finance Committee Act the cost of a tea garden plant was kept at 30 to 50 per cent. The return on investment was introduced in 1976 at a rate of 25%.This compensation became effective in the assessment year 1991-92 for the cost of new plant and machinery. The Investment Deposit Accounting Scheme was introduced in 1986.Some amount is deducted from the amount deposited in this compensation. The development bank deposits are used for the purpose of purchasing a new ship, new aircraft or new machinery plant, purchasing a computer or repaying the annual loan amount. The scheme became effective in the assessment year 1991-92.

Yet even if the concessions were excluded the number of concessions still continued to be large. Yet even if the concessions were excluded the number of concessions still continued to be large.

1.   Charities to specific funds, charitable organizations, etc.

The charity was created for a special fund (The charity was created for a special fund) and organizations (Such as colleges or best national institutions, national foundations community dialogue etc.) In some cases 100 per cent of the total income and in some cases 50 per cent of the income is deducted. Some taxes have no limit on charities and some taxes have a limit of 10 percent of total profits.

2.   Charities for scientific research or rural development:

Any amount for the implementation of scientific research in a company or institution, college or college for any rural development programs in any organization or society that takes responsibility for natural resource afforestation or conservation programs. Deduction is deducted from the total income by the Central Government for setting up any fund for afforestation or for setting up a fund for rural development by the Central Government.

3.   **Deduction is deducted from the total income by the Central Government for setting up any fund for afforestation or for setting up a fund for rural development by the Central Government.:**

This criterion is intended to attract capital from backward areas. Under this provision, 20 per cent of the profits and benefits associated with new industries or for setting up hotel industry in backward areas etc. are deducted from the total profits.

4.   Profits and benefits under newly established small-sized industrial units in certain areas:

Under this provision, 20 per cent of the profits and benefits from newly established small scale in rural areas are deducted from the total income. This facility has been designed for new small scale businesses for a period of 10 years.

5.   Profits and benefits through projects outside India:

Under this provision 50 per cent of the profit is deducted from the benefits received by the project operating outside India.

6.   Profit retained for export business:

Under this provision the company is engaged in export business. Export of goods is deducted from the profit received. These benefits are shared by those who support the producers.

7. Earnings in convertible foreign exchange:

Under this provision, the Indian company is mostly engaged in hotel business, travel planner or travel agent.50 per cent of their profits are deducted after they are provided for the services of foreign tourists and the amount deducted is converted into foreign exchange in India.

8.   Profit through export of computer software:

Under this provision, only the profits generated by Indian companies generated by computer software experts are deducted from the development revenue and converted into foreign exchange.

9.   Profits and benefits through industrial liability after a certain time:

Under this provision 25 per cent of the profits are deducted from the total amount in industries like newly started industrial liability, shipping and hotel business etc. In addition, if such companies were started in 1990-91, they are deducted 30 per cent under sub-section 80-1.

10.   Profits and benefits under industrial liability:

Under this section, when a company enters a new venture, it assumes responsibility for the industrial backward area in the state or central sector (Which was started production from 1-4-1993) they are given 100 per cent after the first 5 years and 30 per cent after the second 5 years. The company is bound to give concessions for uniform production and distribution.

11.   Profits and benefits through poultry farming business:

33 1 /3 is deducted from the profit earned from poultry farming. Under this section, when the is calculated, the total income is also calculated.

12.   Inter-corporate dividends:

Dividends paid by the company under this section are deducted. Authorized Banks, Financial Institutions, State Financial Corporations, State Industrial Investments or Registered Companies are allowed to deduct 60% of the income received in the form of dividends under Section 25 of the Companies Act.

13.   Royalties by certain foreign companies:

Under this section, up to 50 per cent is deducted from income converted into foreign exchange in India on income from royalties, patents, model design, technical or business services, etc.

14.   Profits and benefits from the publication of books:

Under this section 20 per cent of the profit is deducted from the print business and its amount from published books.

(5)   The collapse of the tax base and Zero tax companies:

Deficits in government revenue have led to the collapse of the tax base and the main reason is tax breaks. In addition to concessions, some returns also play an important role in creating a deficit. Some of these returns, such as depreciation returns and investment returns from 1990, are for future years. If the depreciation compensation is more than the declared income of the company in the current year, the company gets more profit and pays higher dividends to shareholders. If the company declares itself as zero tax, the company is completely exempt from corporation tax.

The CMIE (Central Monitoring of Indian Economy) surveyed 200 companies stating that in 1994-95, when companies earned 80 per cent of their profits, 45 per cent of their profits were not taxed. In addition, the Ministry of Finance Government of India surveyed 1000 companies and observed that the additional annual income was Rs 3600 crore and clarified that zero tax companies are taxed as per the minimum alternative tax. Zero tax companies that do not pay corporation tax and make a profit for reasons of income and equality are not appropriate. Examining this problem, it was introduced under the Income Tax Act 1961-80 and came into force in 1984.The law prohibits 70 per cent of the total deductions from the total income before the incentives and at least 30 per cent tax was levied on the company's income. This law was replaced by a new law introduced in 1987 under 115.There was a provision to levy 30 per cent corporation tax on book profits. Most companies calculate the tax under income tax law in which 30 per cent of the book profit is levied. But this provision was repealed in 1990.The investment return was then canceled and the tax base improved. The incentives declined as expected but the additional reduction in incentives did not offset the collapse of the tax base.

When a minimum tax was imposed on zero tax companies it became a topic of much discussion. One idea is that a minimum income tax is required and that it is property based. One idea is that a minimum income tax is required and that it is property based. He also said that the idea of minimum tax is required to get 5 to 10 per cent on profits after interest but should not be more than 20 per cent of pre-depreciation and book profits. Often where there is no profit there are many practical difficulties in levying the minimum alternative tax but it is the best and efforts have been made to keep the restructuring of incentives as far away as possible. Because the increase in incentives is considered to be a big reason for the emergence of a zero tax company. The decline in the tax base could have been prevented if the incentives had been reduced, but the grounds for reviving the incentive structure were found to be stronger than the minimum tax.

The Central Board of Direct Taxes has issued the following guidelines for monitoring mandatory tax returns for companies:

1.   All companies with a turnover of Rs 100 crore in Mumbai and Rs 25 crore in others.

2.   Publicly issued companies with an income of Rs 1 crore should be included in the list of compulsory inspection tax returns.

3.   To change the book profit of a company by Rs 10 lakh if the income tax return of the total income is less than 50 per cent.

4.   When companies increase their share of capital or have unsecured loans of Rs 1 crore or more in a year, compare it with the previous year.

Major post-1991 reforms:

As per the main resolution of the 1994 Act, there are differences between some existing domestic companies. It is divided into large dominant companies and narrow dominant companies. Again, after the 1991 resolution of the Finance Act, domestic companies were classified into two parts. Industrial and Commercial Companies The tax rate of industrial companies is lower than the tax rate of non-industrial companies. The 1994-95 budgets distinguished between a large dominant company and a narrow dominant one. A surcharge of 15 per cent has been maintained since the tax rate was abolished from 40 per cent for all domestic companies and the effective tax rate has been reduced to 46 per cent.

In the 1996-97 budgets, the surcharge rate for domestic companies was reduced from 15 per cent to 7.5 per cent. In the 1997-98 budgets, the surcharge on companies was completely abolished and the tax rate for domestic companies was reduced from 40 per cent to 35 per cent. In 1999-2000, domestic companies and firms were forced to levy a surcharge of 10 per cent. The surcharge rate for the financial year 2001-02 was 2 per cent.

(3)   Minimum Alternative Tax:

India has a minimum alternative tax on having companies. India has a minimum alternative tax on companies. "A company that pays a minimum tax under the Income Tax Act due to the amount of concessions and tax choice is called a zero tax company' 'The first attempt at this tax was made in 1983 for companies under Section 80 of the Income Tax Act(1961).

Normally it is the responsibility of the company to pay tax on the calculated income as per the provisions of the Income Tax Act but as per the provisions of the Companies Act the company prepares the profit and loss account of the company itself. Taxes are not paid because income is negligible or negative or meaningless when calculating on income according to income tax law. In such circumstances the company declares its book profit and declares the dividend paid to the shareholders in which the companies have not paid income tax. Such companies are referred to as zero tax companies. These companies were assessed under the Income Tax Act in the year 1997-98.In this section, the taxable tax calculated by the company under this Act is less than 30% of the next year 1996-97 and its book profit is equal to 30% of the book profit of the amount related to the taxable year of the total income of such companies.

The new tax credit scheme was introduced through a minimum alternative tax. Some conditions were introduced during the five years to apply this regular tax which are as follows:

1. When a company pays tax under MAT, it also earns an amount of tax credit, which is the difference between income tax payable and regular tax.

2. According to the MAT credit, a period of 5 years is allowed in the assessment year in which the tax is paid.

3. There is a difference between the regular tax and the tax calculated under the law when the regular tax becomes payable in the assessment year.

4. Credit is allowed without incurring any interest.

During the financial year 2000, this Act was introduced in Section 115-B under the Income Tax Act, 1961 with effect from 1-4-01.For example, in the assessment year 2001-02, a minimum alternative tax was levied on companies. Therefore, according to the new provision of Act 115-B, if the book is less than 7.5 per cent of the profit and tax is payable from the total income, then 7.5 per cent of the book profit is paid under this provision. The Fiscal Act was introduced in the financial year 2005-06 to 2006-07, which was taxed at less than 7.5 per cent of book profits. In the 2010-11 budget, MAT has increased by 18 per cent under 115-JB.

Book profit: Book profit is the net profit that a company keeps in its records.

Calculation of Book Profit : Book profit is the net profit which is shown in the profit and loss account for the following year.

- Amount of income tax paid or payable

- Taking the amounts to any reserve (Special reserves under 33 AC section)

- Indefinite liability other than to establish the amount of provision made for the liability received

- Amount by provision for losses of subsidiaries or

- The amount of dividend paid or estimated or

- Any amount of income related to expenses that applies under Section 10 or Section 10 or 10A or Section 10B or Section 11 or Section 12 or

- The amount of depreciation (Was introduced by the Finance Act 2006).

Chapter -4

Analysis of Corporate Tax

This chapter is informed by an analytical study of corporation taxes.

1. Data of Year wise

2. Data of state wise

Corporation tax is a tax levied on the income of a company in which the figures before 1991 and after 1991 show that the corporation tax appears to increase as the income of companies increases and remains stable after a few years and then decreases

Table-1

Contribution of corporation tax to the total tax revenue of the Central Government

In crore.

Year	Corporation Tax (Rs.Crore)	Corporation Tax (% change)	Corporation Tax (% of gross tax revenue)	Corporation Tax (% of total receipts)
1979-80	1392	-	11.59	9.03
1980-81	1377	-1.10	10.47	7.03
1981-82	1970	43.10	12.46	8.57
1982-83	2185	10.90	12.35	7.79
1983-84	2493	14.10	12.03	7.31
1984-85	2556	2.50	10.89	6.41
1985-86	2865	12.10	9.99	6.05
1986-87	3160	10.30	9.62	5.78
1987-88	3433	8.60	**9.11**	5.50
1988-89	4407	28.40	9.91	6.00

1989-90	4729	0.30	9.16	5.40
1990-91	5335	12.80	9.27	5.68
2000-01	35696	16.30	18.93	10.92
2001-02	36609	2.60	19.57	10.06
2002-03	46172	26.10	21.35	11.22
2003-04	63562	37.70	24.99	13.38
2004-05	82680	30.10	27.11	16.33
2005-06	101277	22.50	27.66	19.23
2006-07	144318	42.50	30.48	24.93
2007-08	192911	33.70	32.52	26.07
2008-09	213395	10.60	35.25	25.41
2009-10	244725	14.68	**39.19**	23.56
2010-11	298688	18.07	37.66	25.08
2011-12	322816	7.47	36.31	24.45
2012-13	356326	9.40	34.39	24.38
2013-14	394678	9.72	34.66	25.00

2014-15	428925	7.98	34.45	27.05
2015-16	453228	5.36	31.14	25.50
2016-17	484924	6.54	28.26	24.44
2017-18	571202	15.10	29.77	26.72
2018-19	663572	13.92	31.90	30.18
2019-20(R)	610500	8.69	28.22	23.68
2020-21 (B)	681000	10.35	28.11	22.42

(Source: Union Budget 2019-20)

Corporation Tax (Rs.Crore)

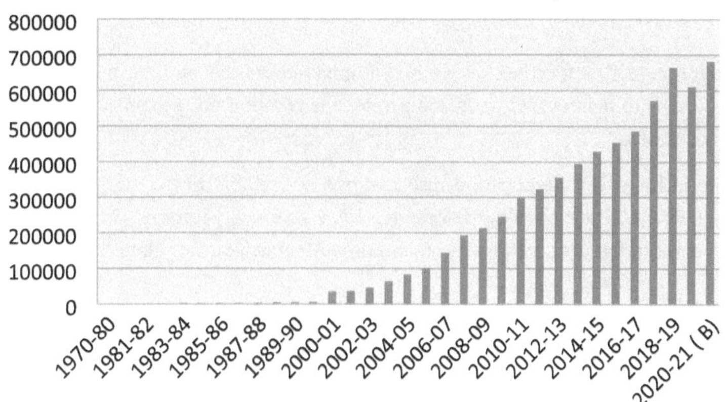

Corporation Tax (% change) -

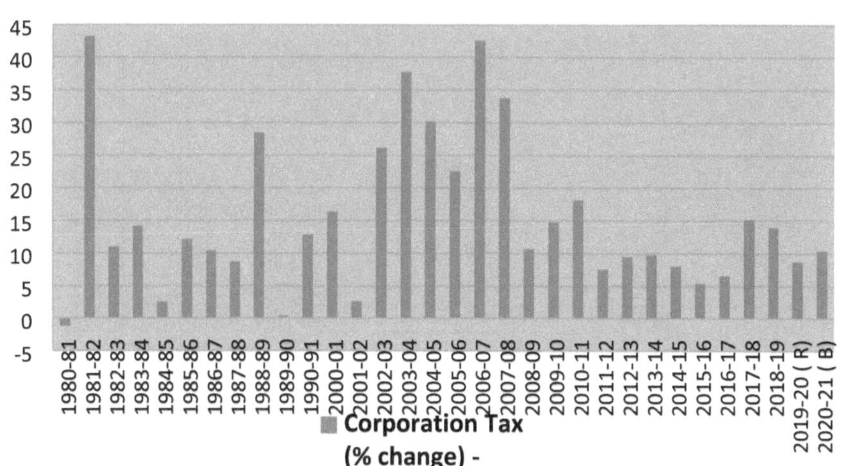

As mentioned in the table above, the corporation tax levied by the government seems to be increasing. In some years the corporation tax seems to increase while in some years the corporation tax appears to be low and stable and in some years it decreases.

Before the 1991 economic reforms, liberalization, privatization and globalization, corporation tax revenues did not improve as much as they should. Before the 1991 economic reforms, liberalization, privatization and globalization, corporation tax revenues did not improve as much as they should.

Table -2

YEAR	Corporation Tax(rs.Crore)
1979-80	1392
1990-91	5335
2011-12	322816
2020-21	681000

Corporation Tax(rs.Crore)

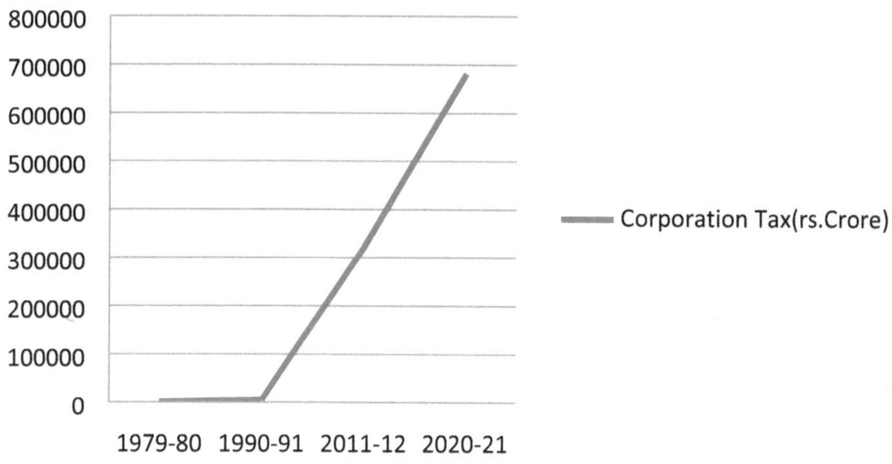

Table -3

YEAR	Corporation Tax (% of gross tax revenue)
1979-80	11.59
1990-91	9.27
2011-12	36.31
2020-21	28.11

Corporation Tax (% of gross tax revenue)

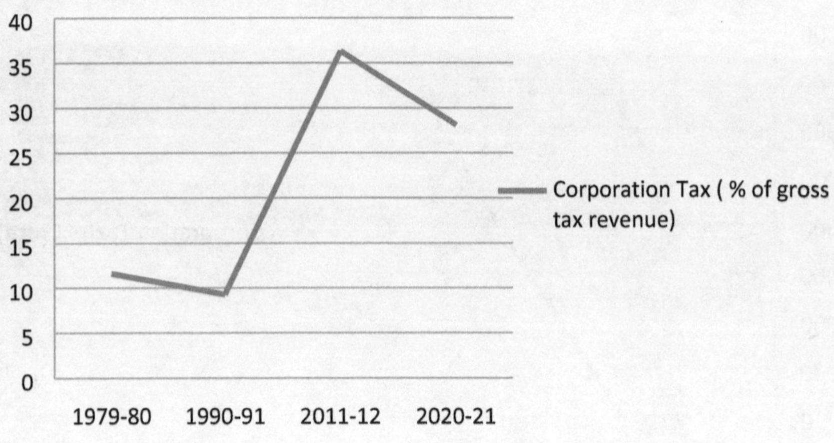

Table-4

YEAR	Corporation Tax (% of Total Receipts)
1979-80	9.03
1990-91	5.68
2011-12	24.45
2020-21	22.42

Corporation Tax (% of Total Receipts)

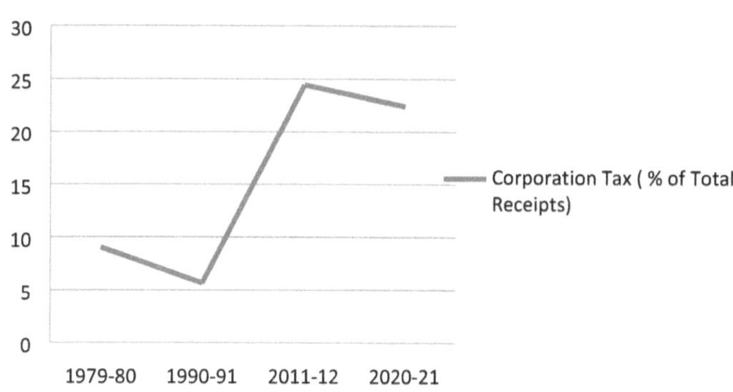

Based on the above information, the government collected corporation tax of Rs. 1392 crore in the year 1979-80. In the year 1970-71, the total tax revenue was Rs 3207 crore, of which the share of corporation tax was Rs 371 crore. In the year 1980-81, the total tax collection was Rs. 13320 crore out of which the corporation tax was Rs. 1311 crore. The corporation tax was reduced by -1.1 per cent as compared to the previous year. Similarly, the share of corporation tax in 1981-82 was Rs. 1970 crore in which the corporation tax was changed by 43.1 per cent as compared to the previous year. Similarly, in the year 1982-83, the corporation tax collection was Rs. 2185 crore which was reduced by 12.9 per cent. In the year 1983-84, the corporation tax collection was Rs. 2493 crore, which was a change of 14.1 per cent over the previous year. The year 1984-85 saw a share of Rs 2,556 crore in corporation tax with a change of 2.5 per cent. Similarly, in the year 1985-86, the corporation tax collection was Rs. 2865 crore and the share of total tax revenue from 1980-81 to 1984-85 was 10.7 per cent, 12.46 per cent, 12.35 per cent, 12.03 per cent and 10.89 per cent respectively.

In 1986-87, the corporation tax contribution was Rs 3,160 crore, a change of 10.3 per cent over the previous year. And the share of corporation tax in total tax revenue was 9.62 per cent. In the year 1987-88, the collection of corporation tax was Rs 3433 crore with a change of 8.6 per cent and the share of corporation tax in the total tax was 9.11 per cent. In the year 1988-89, the corporation tax was Rs 4407 crore and its contribution to the total tax was 9.91 per cent and the change was 28.4 per cent. In the year 1989-90, the corporation tax collection was Rs. 4729 crore, which was reduced by 7.3 per cent over the previous year. And the share of corporation tax in total tax revenue was 9.16 per cent.

After the economic reforms after 1991, the collection of corporation tax increased and the contribution of corporation tax to the total tax revenue also decreased. In the year 1990-91, the corporation tax was levied at Rs. 5335 crore out of which the total tax revenue was Rs. 57513 crore. Looking at the year-on-year data, it seems that as the total tax revenue increases, so does its corporate tax revenue.

After the economic reforms of 1991, the corporation tax in the year 2001-02 was Rs 36609 crore while the share of total tax was Rs 186374 crore. The share of corporation tax in total tax was 19.57 per cent and the percentage change in corporation tax was 2.6 per cent which is considered very negligible. In the year 2002-03, the corporation tax was Rs 46666 crore and the share of corporation tax in the total tax was 21.35 per cent while the percentage change in corporation tax was 26.1 per cent. In the year 2003-04, the corporation tax was Rs 63562 crore, the share of total tax was Rs 252748 crore and the share of corporation tax in the total tax was 24.99 per cent.As well as the percentage change of corporation tax was 30.1 per cent and the share of corporation tax in the total tax was 27.11 per cent. In the year 2005-06, the total tax collection was Rs 363,326 crore out of which the corporation tax revenue was Rs 10,177 crore. Of the total tax, the corporation tax revenue was 27.66 per cent and the percentage change in the corporation tax was 22.5 per cent. The total tax revenue in the year 2006-07 was Rs.471512 crore out of which the corporation tax revenue was Rs.144318 crore. As well as the share of corporation tax in total tax was 30.48 per cent and the percentage change in corporation tax was 42.50 per cent which increased.

Total tax revenue in the year 2007-08 was Rs. 591347 crore out of which corporation tax revenue was Rs. 191911 crore. And the share of corporation tax in the total tax was 32.52 per cent As well as a percentage change in the corporation tax was 33.7 percent. This was less than the previous year. The corporate tax rate this year was 33.66 percent. In the year 2008-09, the total tax revenue was Rs 603499 crore while the share of corporation tax in the total tax was 35.25 per cent. And the percentage change in the corporation tax was 10.6 per cent which was reduced. The total tax revenue in the year 2009-10 was Rs. 621368 crore out of which the corporation tax revenue was Rs. 244725 crore. Corporation tax accounted for 39.19 per cent of the total tax. As well as a percentage change in the corporation tax was 14.7 percent. The central government introduced a new direct tax code in the year 2009-10 which also gave more relief to the corporate sector. Provision was also made for a corporate tax of 25 per cent. Direct tax revenue grew by 15 per cent this year.

Provision was made to abolish surcharge and cess on corporate tax in the year 2009-10.As well as the corporate tax rate was kept at 30 per cent and the minimum alternative tax was kept at 20 per cent of the book profits of the companies. Again in the budget, it was proposed that the direct tax code would come into force from April 1, 2012 and if corporate tax was levied without any surcharge and cess, it would exceed 33 per cent. Thus, the corporate tax rate (including surcharge and cess) was about 33.22 per cent this year. In the year 2010-11, the total tax revenue was Rs 793072 crore out of which the corporation tax revenue was Rs 298688 crore. While the corporation tax was 37.66 per cent and the percentage change in the corporation tax was 18.07 per cent. Also, the surcharge on corporate tax was likely to be abolished this year and the minimum alternative tax was raised from 18 per cent to 20 per cent.

In the year 2011-12, the total tax revenue was Rs 889177 crore and the corporation tax revenue was Rs 322816 crore and the share of corporation tax in the total tax was 36.31 per cent and the percentage change in corporation tax was 7.47 per cent. This was less than the previous year. In the year 2012-13, the total tax revenue was Rs 1036235 crore and the corporation tax revenue was Rs 356326 crore while the share of corporation tax in the total tax was 34.39 per cent and the percentage change in corporation tax was 9.4 per cent. In 2013-14, the total tax revenue was Rs 1138733 crore, of which the corporation tax revenue was Rs 394678 crore. The share of corporation tax in the total tax was 34.66 per cent and the percentage change in corporation tax was 9.72 per cent. In the year 2014-15, the total tax revenue was Rs 1244886 crore and the corporation tax revenue was Rs 428925 crore. The share of corporation tax in the total tax was 34.45 per cent. And the percentage change in the corporation tax was 7.98 per cent which was reduced.

In the year 2015-16, the total tax revenue was Rs 1455648 crore and the corporation tax revenue was Rs 453228 crore. Also, the share of corporation tax in the total tax was 31.14 per cent and the percentage change in corporation tax was 5.36 per cent which was less than the previous year. In the year 2016-17, the total tax revenue was Rs 1715822 crore out of which the corporation tax revenue was Rs 484924 crore. Also, the share of corporation tax in total tax was 25.26 per cent and the percentage change in corporation tax was 6.54 per cent which has increased. In the year 2017-18, the total tax revenue was Rs 1919008 crore and the corporation tax revenue was Rs 571202 crore. The share of corporation tax in total tax was 29.77 per cent and the percentage change in corporation tax was 15.1 per cent which is higher than the previous year. In the year 2018-19, the total tax revenue was Rs 2080465 crore and the corporation tax revenue was Rs 663572 crore. The share of corporation tax in the total tax was 31.9 per cent and the percentage change in corporation tax was 13.92 per cent which was less. In the year 2019-20, the total tax revenue was Rs 2163423 crore and the corporation tax revenue was Rs 610500 crore. The share of corporation tax in total tax was 28.22 per cent and the percentage change in corporation tax was 8.69 per cent which is less than the previous year. Total tax revenue in the year 2020-21 was Rs.2423020 crore and corporation tax revenue was Rs.681000 crore As well, the share of corporation tax in total tax was 28.11 per cent and the percentage change in corporation tax was 10.35 per cent which has increased.

Thus, from the analysis of statistics, it can be seen that as the total direct tax revenue has increased, so has the corporation tax revenue But the percentage change in the corporation tax is seen differently every year.

Table-5
State-based corporation tax share

No	State	2011-12	2012-13	2013-14	2014-15	2015-16	2016-17	2017-18
1		66.18	69.89	75.57	47.51	76.33	81.35	96.21
2	Arunachal Pradesh	3.13	3.30	3.57	3.85	24.29	25.89	30.62
3	Assam	34.61	36.55	39.52	42.62	58.71	62.57	73.99
4	Bihar	104.15	109.99	118.93	128.24	171.37	182.63	216.00
5	Chhattisgarh	23.57	24.89	26.90	29.01	54.61	58.20	68.83
6	Goa	2.54	2.68	2.90	3.12	6.70	7.14	8.44
7	Gujarat	29.01	30.64	33.13	35.72	54.68	58.27	68.92

8	Haryana	9.99	10.56	11.42	12.31	19.22	20.48	24.22
9	Himachal Pradesh	7.45	7.87	8.51	9.17	12.64	13.47	15.93
10	Jammu & Kashmir	14.79	15.63	16.90	18.22	32.87	35.03	41.44
11	Jharkhand	26.73	28.23	30.52	32.92	55.65	59.32	70.15
12	Karnataka	41.29	43.60	47.15	50.84	83.57	89.05	105.33
13	Kerala	22.33	23.59	25.50	27.50	44.32	47.24	55.87
14	Madhya Pradesh	67.93	71.74	77.56	83.64	133.83	142.63	168.70
15	Maharashtra	49.60	52.38	56.64	61.07	97.89	104.33	123.39
16	Manipur	4.30	4.54	4.91	5.30	10.94	11.66	13.79
17	Meghalaya	3.89	4.11	4.44	4.79	11.38	12.13	14.35
18	Mizoram	2.56	2.71	2.93	3.16	8.16	8.69	10.28
19	Nagaland	2.99	3.16	3.42	3.69	8.83	9.41	11.13
20	Odisha	45.59	48.15	52.06	56.14	82.30	87.72	103.74
21	Punjab	13.25	13.99	15.13	16.32	27.96	29.80	35.24
22	Rajasthan	55.84	58.97	63.76	68.76	97.43	103.84	122.81
23	Sikkim	2.28	2.40	2.60	2.81	6.50	6.94	-
24	Tamil nadu	47.40	50.06	54.13	58.37	71.33	76.02	-
25	Telangana	-	-	-	33.98	43.21	46.05	54.46

2 6	Tripura	4.88	5.15	5.57	6.00	11.38	12.13	14.35
2 7	Uttar Pradesh	187.73	198.26	214.35	231.15	318.43	339.36	401.37
2 8	Uttrakhand	10.69	11.28	12.20	13.16	18.65	19.88	23.51
2 9	West Bengal	69.30	73.19	79.13	85.33	129.86	138.39	163.68

Table 5.1

No.	State	2018-19	2019-20	2020-21
1	Andhra Pradesh	104.88	95.35	99.16
2	Arunachal Pradesh	33.38	30.35	42.45
3	Assam	80.66	73.34	75.52
4	Bihar	235.46	214.08	242.68
5	Chhattisgarh	75.03	68.22	82.45
6	Goa	9.21	8.37	9.31
7	Gujarat	75.13	68.31	81.96
8	Haryana	26.40	24.01	26.09
9	Himachal Pradesh	17.37	15.79	19.27
10	Jammu & Kashmir	45.17	41.07	-
11	Jharkhand	76.47	69.53	79.91
12	Karnataka	114.82	104.39	87.95
13	Kerala	60.90	55.38	46.87
14	Madhya Pradesh	183.88	167.19	190.22
15	Maharashtra	134.50	122.30	147.98
16	Manipur	15.03	13.67	17.31
17	Meghalaya	15.64	14.22	18.45
18	Mizoram	11.21	10.19	12.21
19	Nagaland	12.13	11.03	13.82
20	Odisha	113.09	102.82	111.66
21	Punjab	38.42	34.93	43.13
22	Rajasthan	133.87	121.72	144.22
23	Sikkim	8.94	8.13	9.36
24	Tamil nadu	98.00	89.11	101.04
25	Telangana	59.37	53.98	51.45

26	Tripura	15.64	14.22	17.10
27	Uttar Pradesh	437.51	397.81	432.52
28	Uttrakhand	25.63	23.30	26.63
29	West Bengal	178.43	162.23	181.37

Source: Budget 2011-12 and 2020-21

Chart

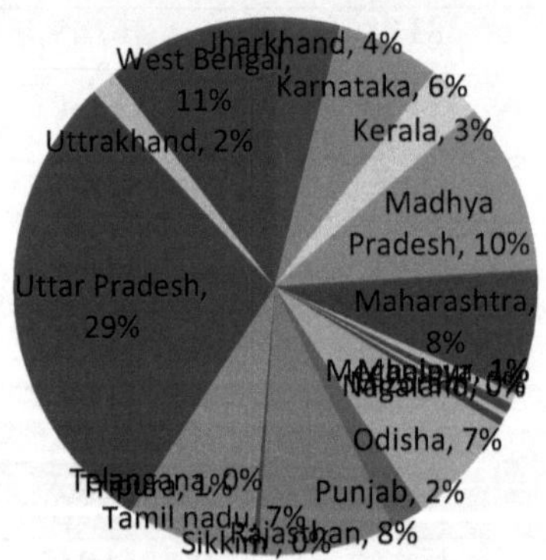

Table-6

State	2011-12	2020-21
Andhra Pradesh	66.18	99.16
Arunachal Pradesh	3.13	42.45
Assam	34.61	75.52
Bihar	104.15	242.68
Chhattisgarh	23.57	82.45
Goa	2.54	9.31
Gujarat	29.01	81.96
Haryana	9.99	26.09
Himachal Pradesh	7.45	19.27
Jammu and Kashmir	14.79	-
Jharkhand	26.73	79.91
Karnataka	41.29	87.95
Kerala	22.33	46.87
Madhya Pradesh	67.93	190.22
Maharashtra	49.60	147.98
Manipur	4.30	17.31
Meghalaya	3.89	18.45
Mizoram	2.56	12.21
Nagaland	2.99	13.82
Odisha	45.59	111.66
Punjab	13.25	43.13
Rajasthan	55.84	144.22
Sikkim	2.28	9.36
Tamil nadu	47.40	101.04
Telangana	-	51.45
Tripura	4.88	17.10
Uttar Pradesh	187.73	432.52
Uttrakhand	10.69	26.63
West Bengal	69.30	181.37

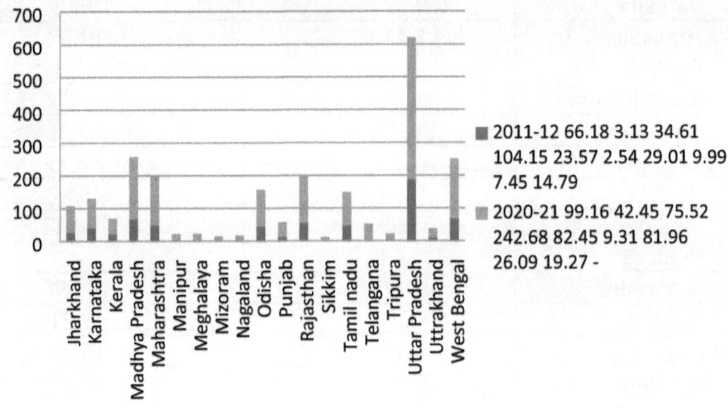

Looking at the table above, it appears that the corporation tax revenue varies from state to state. As well as the corporation tax is increasing every year statewide. As well as the corporation tax is increasing every year statewide. Uttar Pradesh is the highest corporation tax payer in 2011-12 and Sikkim is the lowest tax payer. This year, 187.73 per cent in Uttar Pradesh and 2.28 per cent in Sikkim were corporation tax evasion. In 2012-13, the highest corporation tax collection was 198.26 per cent in Uttar Pradesh and the lowest was 2.4

per cent in Sikkim. In 2013-14, the highest tax collection was 214.35 per cent in Uttar Pradesh and the lowest was 2.6 per cent in Sikkim. In 2014-15, Uttar Pradesh, the highest corporation-paying state, had a tax collection of 231.15 per cent, followed by Sikkim at 2.81 per cent. In 2015-16, Uttar Pradesh had the highest tax collection at 318.43 per cent and Sikkim had the lowest at 6.5 per cent.

In 2016-17, Uttar Pradesh had the highest corporation tax collection at 339.36 per cent and Sikkim had the lowest at 6.94 per cent. In 2017-18, the highest corporate income was 401.37 per cent in Uttar Pradesh and the lowest income was 8.44 per cent in Goa.In 2018-19, Uttar Pradesh had the highest corporation tax revenue of 437.51 per cent and Sikkim had the lowest at 8.94 per cent. In the year 2019-20, Uttar Pradesh has 397.81 per cent corporation tax revenue and Sikkim has 8.13 per cent less revenue. In the year 2020-21, the corporate revenue collection is 432.52 per cent in Uttar Pradesh and 9.31 per cent in Goa.

Direct taxes are collected mainly by the Central Government as follows:

Central Government Main Taxes

1. Income Tax

2. Corporation Tax

3. Wealth Tax

4. Custom

5. Excise Duty

6. Service Tax

7. Capital Tax

8. Expenditure Tax

9. Estate Duty

10. Gift Tax

11. Taxes of Union Territories

Table-7

Year	Corporation Tax	Taxes on Income	Interest Tax	Expenditure Tax	Customs
1986-87	3160	2879	0	0	11475
1987-88	3433	3192	0	6	13702
1988-89	4407	4241	0	42	15805
1989-90	4729	5010	0	75	18036
1990-91	5335		-1	82	20644
2001-02	36609	32004	189	261	40268
2002-03	46172	36866	-275	170	44852
2003-04	63562	41387	-46	50	48629
2004-05	82680	49268	50	36	57611
2005-06	101277	55985	13	31	65067
2006-07	144318	75093	5	62	86327
2007-08	192911	102644	3	38	104119
2008-09	213395	106046	9	18	99879
2009-10	244725	122370	9	-62	83324
2010-11	298688	139069	4	29	135813
2011-12	322816	164485	3	21	149328

2012-13	356326	196512	6	15	165346
2013-14	394678	237817	8	9	172085
2014-15	428925	258326	6	11	188016
2015-16	453228	287628	5	4	210338
2016-17	484924	349436	5	15163	225370
2017-18	571202	419880	4	10888	129030
2018-19	663572	472983	3	16	117813
2019-20	640500	559500	0	0	125000
2020-21	681000	638000	0	0	138000

Table-8

Year	Union Excise Duties	Estate Duty	Wealth Tax	Gift Tax	Taxes of Union Territories	Service Tax	Goods and Service Tax
1986-87	14470	14	174	9	607	0	0
1987-88	16426	8	101	8	723	0	0
1988-89	18841	6	122	7	881	0	0
1989-90	22406	4	179	8	969	0	0
1990-91	24514	3	231	3	1118	0	0
2001-02	72555	1	135	-2	545	3302	0
2002-03	82310	0	154	-2	573	4122	0
2003-04	90774	0	136	1	658	7891	0
2004-05	99125	0	145	2	819	14200	0
2005-06	111226	-1	250	2	1125	23055	0
2006-07	117613	2	240	4	1263	37598	0
2007-08	123611	0	340	2	1324	51301	0
2008-09	108613	1	389	1	1488	60941	0
2009-10	102991	0	505	1	1614	58422	0
2010-11	137701	0	687	0	1982	71016	0
2011-12	144901	0	787	1	2785	97509	0
2012-13	175845	1	844	1	3094	132601	0
2013-14	169455	0	1007	1	3130	154778	0
2014-15	188128	0	1086	0	3204	167969	0
2015-16	288073	1	1079	0	3878	211414	0
2016-17	381756	1	184	0	4146	254499	0
2017-18	258834	1	62	0	4721	81228	442561
2018-19	231045	1	40	0	5592	6904	581559
2019-20	248012	0	0	0	6884	1200	612327
2020-21	267000	0	0	0	7500	1020	690500

Source: Budget 2020-21

The above mentioned taxes are levied by the Central and State Governments. The central government also gets a share of the taxes levied by the central government while some taxes are levied by the state government. The state government also has a share in their income. Moreover, there are some taxes on which the Central Government and the State Government have an equal share.

Now when we talk about corporation tax, corporate tax has been levied the most compared to other taxes.

Table- 9

Year	Corporation Tax	Taxes on Income
1986-87	3160	2879
1987-88	3433	3192
1988-89	4407	4241
1989-90	4729	5010
1990-91	5335	5371
2001-02	36609	32004
2002-03	46172	36866
2003-04	63562	41387
2004-05	82680	49268
2005-06	101277	55985
2006-07	144318	75093
2007-08	192911	102644
2008-09	213395	106046
2009-10	244725	122370
2010-11	298688	139069
2011-12	322816	164485
2012-13	356326	196512
2013-14	394678	237817
2014-15	428925	258326
2015-16	453228	287628
2016-17	484924	349436
2017-18	571202	419880
2018-19	663572	472983
2019-20	640500	559500
2020-21	681000	638000

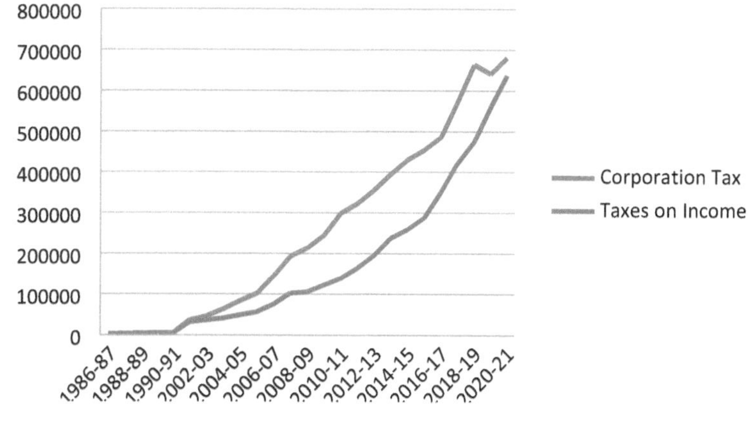

Year	Corporation Tax	Interest Tax
1986-87	3160	0
1987-88	3433	0
1988-89	4407	0
1989-90	4729	0
1990-91	5335	-1
2001-02	36609	189

Year	Corporation Tax	Interest Tax
2002-03	46172	-275
2003-04	63562	-46
2004-05	82680	50
2005-06	101277	13
2006-07	144318	5
2007-08	192911	3
2008-09	213395	9
2009-10	244725	9
2010-11	298688	4
2011-12	322816	3
2012-13	356326	6
2013-14	394678	8
2014-15	428925	6
2015-16	453228	5
2016-17	484924	5
2017-18	571202	4
2018-19	663572	3
2019-20	640500	0
2020-21	681000	0

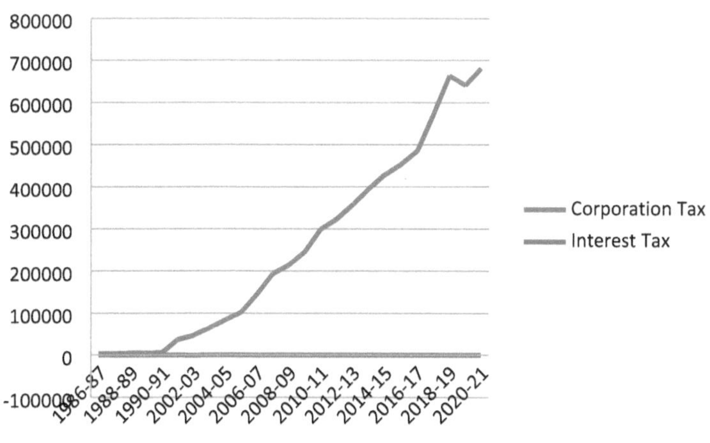

Year	Corporation Tax	Expenditure Tax
1986-87	3160	0
1987-88	3433	6
1988-89	4407	42
1989-90	4729	75
1990-91	5335	82
2001-02	36609	261
2002-03	46172	170
2003-04	63562	50
2004-05	82680	36

2005-06	101277	31
2006-07	144318	62
2007-08	192911	38
2008-09	213395	18
2009-10	244725	-62
2010-11	298688	29
2011-12	322816	21
2012-13	356326	15
2013-14	394678	9
2014-15	428925	11
2015-16	453228	4
2016-17	484924	15163
2017-18	571202	10888
2018-19	663572	16
2019-20	640500	0
2020-21	681000	0

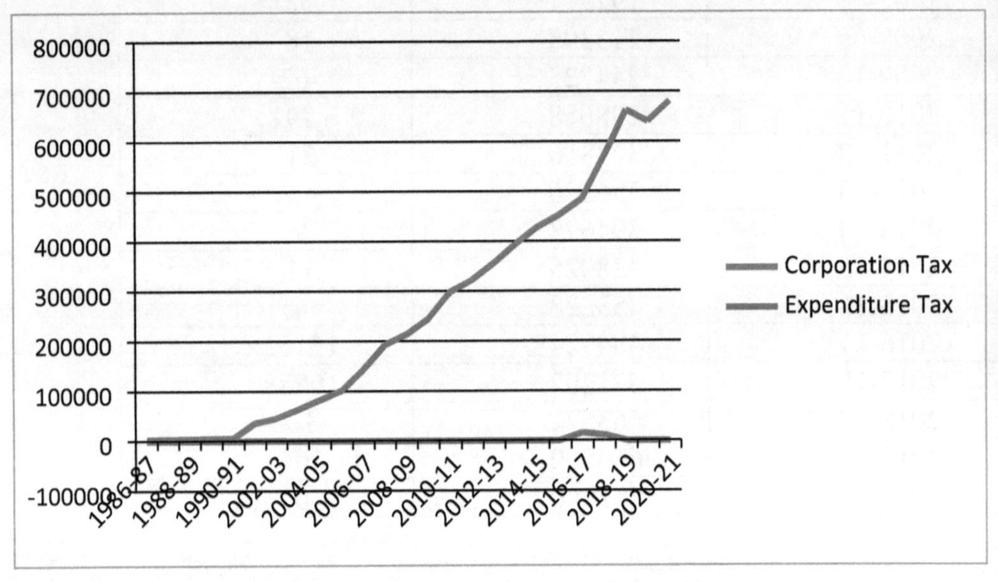

800000
700000
600000
500000
400000
300000
200000
100000
0
-100000
1986-87
1988-89
1990-91
2002-03
2004-05
2006-07
2008-09
2010-11
2012-13
2014-15
2016-17
2018-19
2020-21
Corporation Tax
Expenditure Tax

Year	Corporation Tax	Customs
1986-87	3160	11475
1987-88	3433	13702
1988-89	4407	15805
1989-90	4729	18036
1990-91	5335	20644
2001-02	36609	40268
2002-03	46172	44852
2003-04	63562	48629
2004-05	82680	57611
2005-06	101277	65067
2006-07	144318	86327
2007-08	192911	104119
2008-09	213395	99879
2009-10	244725	83324
2010-11	298688	135813
2011-12	322816	149328
2012-13	356326	165346
2013-14	394678	172085
2014-15	428925	188016
2015-16	453228	210338
2016-17	484924	225370
2017-18	571202	129030
2018-19	663572	117813
2019-20	640500	125000
2020-21	681000	138000

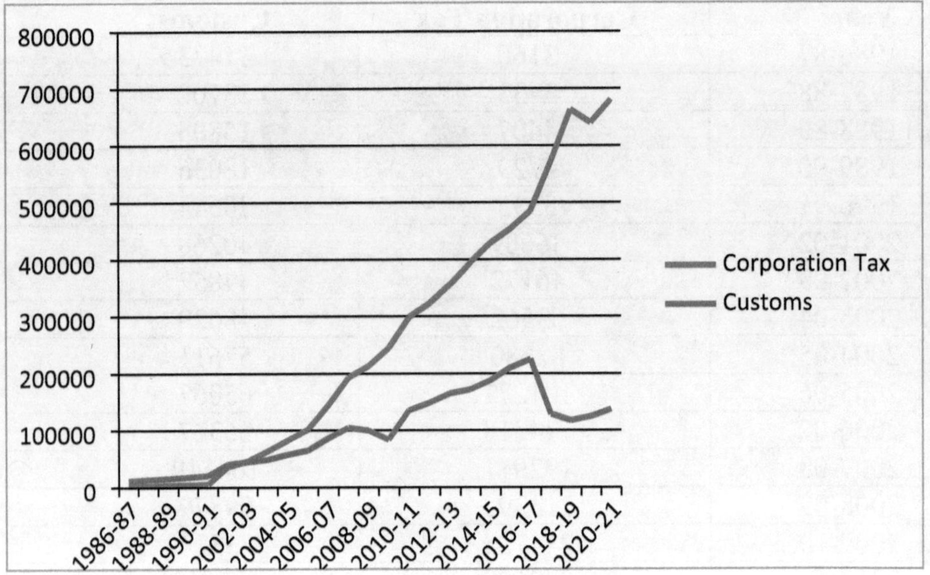

800000
700000
600000
500000
400000
300000
200000
100000
0
Corporation Tax
Customs
1986-87
1988-89
1990-91
2002-03
2004-05
2006-07
2008-09
2010-11
2012-13
2014-15
2016-17
2018-19
2020-21

Year	Corporation Tax	Union Excise Duties
1986-87	3160	14470
1987-88	3433	16426
1988-89	4407	18841
1989-90	4729	22406
1990-91	5335	24514
2001-02	36609	72555
2002-03	46172	82310
2003-04	63562	90774
2004-05	82680	99125
2005-06	101277	111226
2006-07	144318	117613
2007-08	192911	123611
2008-09	213395	108613
2009-10	244725	102991
2010-11	298688	137701
2011-12	322816	144901
2012-13	356326	175845
2013-14	394678	169455
2014-15	428925	188128
2015-16	453228	288073
2016-17	484924	381756
2017-18	571202	258834
2018-19	663572	231045
2019-20	640500	248012
2020-21	681000	267000

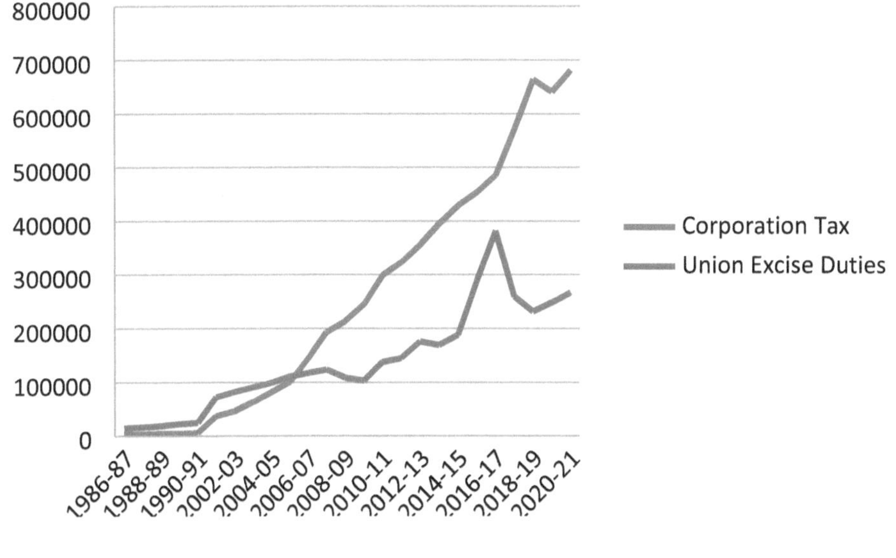

Year	Corporation Tax	Estate Duty
1986-87	3160	14
1987-88	3433	8
1988-89	4407	6
1989-90	4729	4
1990-91	5335	3
2001-02	36609	1
2002-03	46172	0
2003-04	63562	0
2004-05	82680	0
2005-06	101277	-1
2006-07	144318	2
2007-08	192911	0
2008-09	213395	1
2009-10	244725	0
2010-11	298688	0
2011-12	322816	0
2012-13	356326	1
2013-14	394678	0
2014-15	428925	0
2015-16	453228	1
2016-17	484924	1
2017-18	571202	1
2018-19	663572	1
2019-20	640500	0
2020-21	681000	0

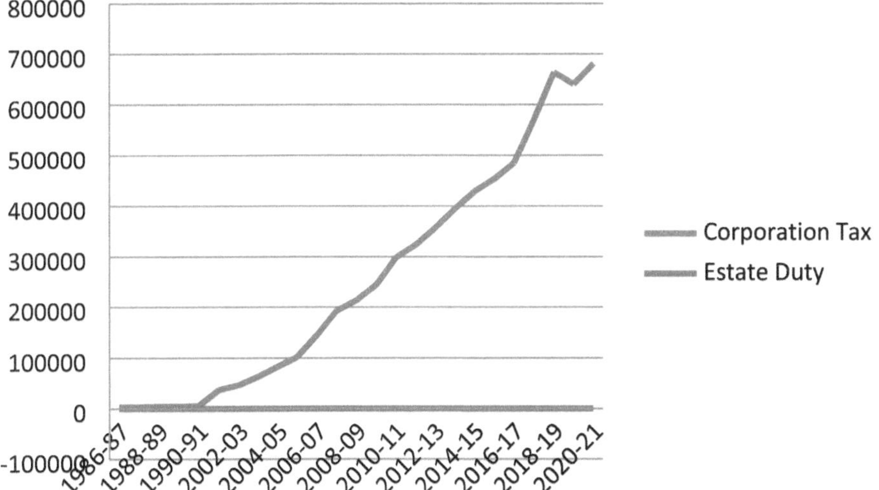

800000
700000
600000
500000
400000
300000
200000
100000
0
-100000
1986-87
1988-89
1990-91
2002-03
2004-05
2006-07
2008-09
2010-11
2012-13
2014-15
2016-17
2018-19
2020-21
Corporation Tax
Estate Duty

Year	Corporation Tax	Wealth Tax
1986-87	3160	174
1987-88	3433	101
1988-89	4407	122
1989-90	4729	179
1990-91	5335	231
2001-02	36609	135
2002-03	46172	154
2003-04	63562	136
2004-05	82680	145
2005-06	101277	250
2006-07	144318	240
2007-08	192911	340
2008-09	213395	389
2009-10	244725	505
2010-11	298688	687
2011-12	322816	787
2012-13	356326	844
2013-14	394678	1007
2014-15	428925	1086
2015-16	453228	1079
2016-17	484924	184
2017-18	571202	62
2018-19	663572	40
2019-20	640500	0
2020-21	681000	0

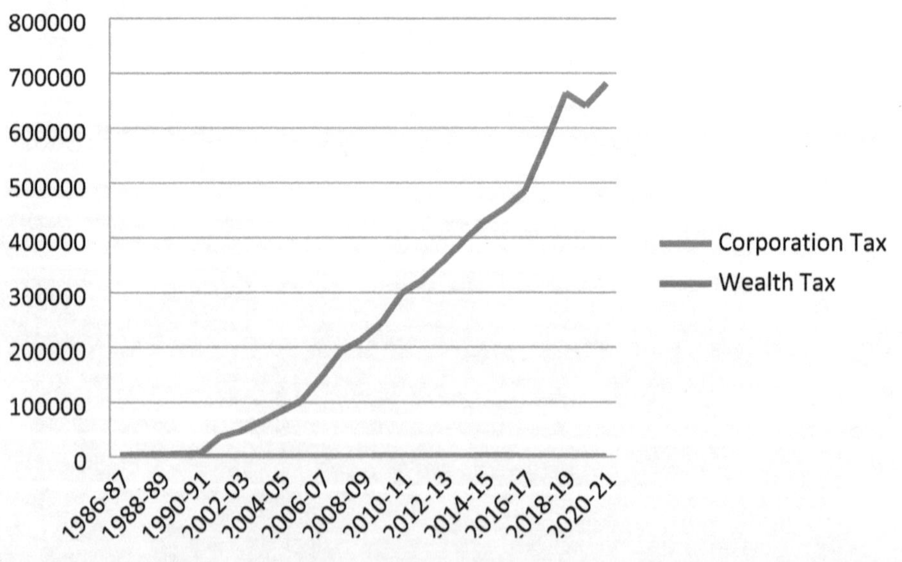

Year	Corporation Tax	Gift Tax
1986-87	3160	9
1987-88	3433	8
1988-89	4407	7
1989-90	4729	8
1990-91	5335	3
2001-02	36609	-2
2002-03	46172	-2
2003-04	63562	1
2004-05	82680	2
2005-06	101277	2
2006-07	144318	4
2007-08	192911	2
2008-09	213395	1
2009-10	244725	1
2010-11	298688	0
2011-12	322816	1
2012-13	356326	1
2013-14	394678	1
2014-15	428925	0
2015-16	453228	0
2016-17	484924	0
2017-18	571202	0
2018-19	663572	0
2019-20	640500	0
2020-21	681000	0

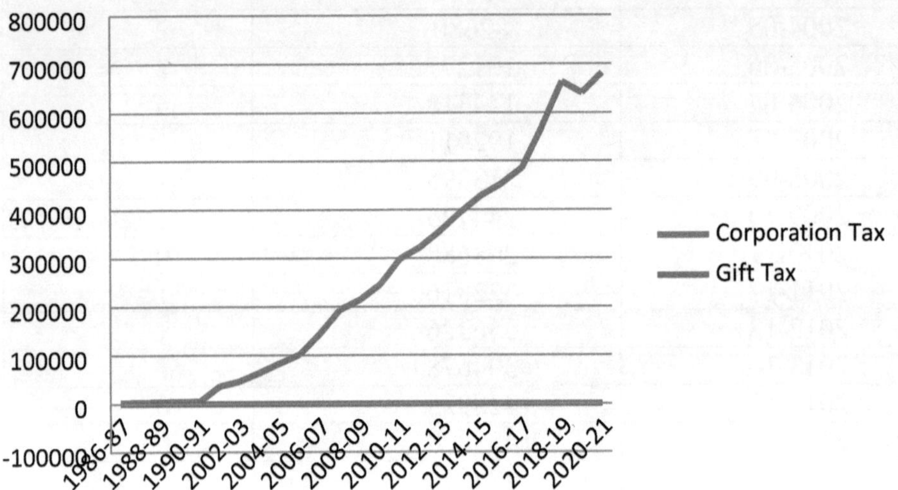

800000
700000
600000
500000
400000
300000
200000
100000
0
-100000
1986-87
1988-89
1990-91
2002-03
2004-05
2006-07
2008-09
2010-11
2012-13
2014-15
2016-17
2018-19
2020-21
Corporation Tax
Gift Tax

Year	Corporation Tax	Taxes of Union Territories
1986-87	3160	607
1987-88	3433	723
1988-89	4407	881
1989-90	4729	969
1990-91	5335	1118
2001-02	36609	545
2002-03	46172	573
2003-04	63562	658
2004-05	82680	819
2005-06	101277	1125
2006-07	144318	1263
2007-08	192911	1324
2008-09	213395	1488
2009-10	244725	1614
2010-11	298688	1982
2011-12	322816	2785
2012-13	356326	3094
2013-14	394678	3130
2014-15	428925	3204
2015-16	453228	3878
2016-17	484924	4146
2017-18	571202	4721
2018-19	663572	5592
2019-20	640500	6884
2020-21	681000	7500

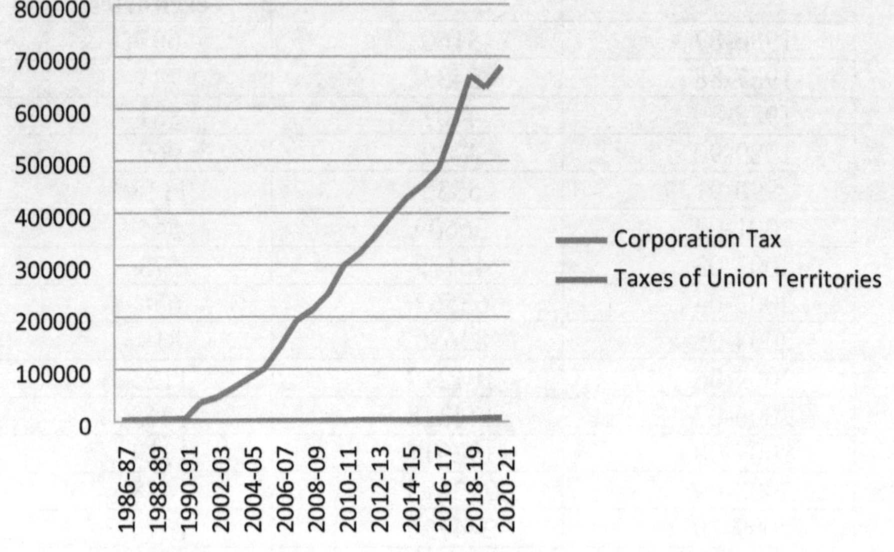
800000
700000
600000
500000
400000
300000
200000
100000
0
1986-87
1988-89
1990-91
2002-03
2004-05
2006-07
2008-09
2010-11
2012-13
2014-15
2016-17
2018-19
2020-21
Corporation Tax
Taxes of Union Territories

Year	Corporation Tax	Service Tax
1986-87	3160	0
1987-88	3433	0
1988-89	4407	0
1989-90	4729	0
1990-91	5335	0
2001-02	36609	3302
2002-03	46172	4122
2003-04	63562	7891
2004-05	82680	14200
2005-06	101277	23055
2006-07	144318	37598
2007-08	192911	51301
2008-09	213395	60941
2009-10	244725	58422
2010-11	298688	71016
2011-12	322816	97509
2012-13	356326	132601
2013-14	394678	154778
2014-15	428925	167969
2015-16	453228	211414
2016-17	484924	254499
2017-18	571202	81228
2018-19	663572	6904
2019-20	640500	1200
2020-21	681000	1020

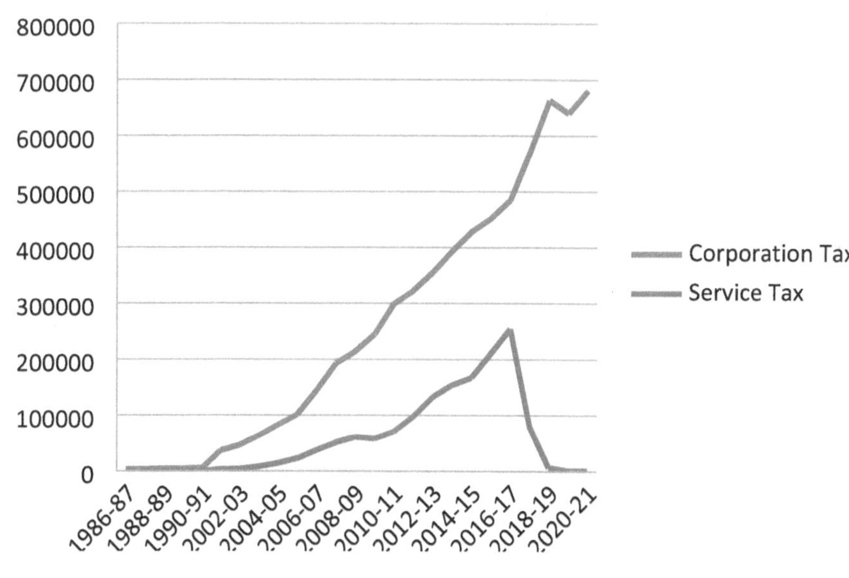

Year	Corporation Tax	Goods and Service Tax
1986-87	3160	0
1987-88	3433	0
1988-89	4407	0
1989-90	4729	0
1990-91	5335	0
2001-02	36609	0
2002-03	46172	0
2003-04	63562	0
2004-05	82680	0
2005-06	101277	0
2006-07	144318	0
2007-08	192911	0
2008-09	213395	0
2009-10	244725	0
2010-11	298688	0
2011-12	322816	0
2012-13	356326	0
2013-14	394678	0
2014-15	428925	0
2015-16	453228	0
2016-17	484924	0
2017-18	571202	442561
2018-19	663572	581559
2019-20	640500	612327
2020-21	681000	690500

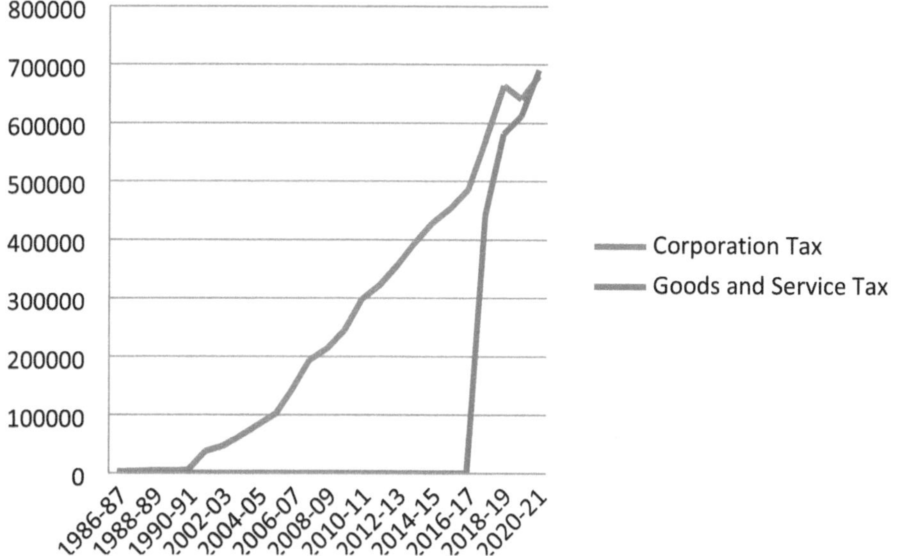

800000
700000
600000
500000
400000
300000
200000
100000
0
1986-87
1988-89
1990-91
2002-03
2004-05
2006-07
2008-09
2010-11
2012-13
2014-15
2016-17
2018-19
2020-21
Corporation Tax
Goods and Service Tax

Chapter- 5

Conclusion

As we have seen, corporation tax is a tax levied on the income of a company and the central government levies direct and indirect taxes.Corporation taxes are included in direct taxes which are collected directly by the government.There has been a lot of controversy over whether the corporation tax burden falls on the company or on the company's shareholders.The Industrial Revolution began in Europe and America in the 1800 centaury and then when the special beginning of this revolution in India, only the first privately owned firms existed.As the business began to grow, a new form of company emerged from the partnership firm.

The company is an artificial entity that exists legally. There were a lot of limitations when it came to private ownership.One person managed and regulated the entire business. There were also limitations to the partnership firm that came into existence.Only a minimum of two members and a maximum of 20 members could enter the partnership firm.But as the industry grew and the business grew, the form of the company came into existence, in which the company was divided with many shareholders.In which the owners of the company are its shareholders and the company is managed by salaried managersbut the shareholders' share in the company's profit and loss is equal to the share they hold.The shareholders who have held more shares in the general meeting of the company have to sit in the general meeting and these members give their consent in the decisions regarding the company.

At present, the currency of the corporate sector in India has increased tremendously.In the present era, new companies have come into existence in India It has competition in telecom, manufacturing, service, marketing, etc.Before independence in India and during the British period, the British set certain criteria for taxation and tax collection.The corporate sector originated during the 18th and 19th centuries.But as the amount of investment increased, so did the number of companies.But as the amount of investment increased, so did the number of companies.But with the increase in investment, its rate could not increase as much as it should.Joint stock companies developed in the subsequent period During World War II and in the post-war period, the number of companies and the investment paid to companies doubled.Then as the corporate sector developed, the corporate sector split into two.Public companies and private companies 'companies in which the public has a special contribution is called a public company 'and 'companies in which certain dominant individuals contribute are called private companies'

But after the economic reforms of 1991, when liberalization, privatization and globalization came, the number of public companies decreased while the number of private companies increased.But after the economic reforms of 1991, when liberalization, privatization and globalization came, the number of public companies decreased while the number of private companies increased.As well as some industries that are newly established are given tax holiday relief for the first five years.However, some are evading taxes, so a new minimum alternative tax rule was introduced under the Income Tax Act from 1997-98.However, some are evading taxes, so a new minimum alternative tax rule was introduced under the Income Tax Act from 1997-98.

Many improvements have been made in the calculation of corporation tax before 1991 and after 1991 including rate structure, revenue income, tax incentives, and erosion of tax base (collapse).Before 1991 and 1960-61 saw very low rates for a very large companyAfter 1991, the rate has been fixed at 40 per cent for broad-based companies and 50 per cent for narrow-dominated companies.After 1991, the rate has been fixed at 40 per cent for broad-based companies and 50 per cent for narrow-dominated companies.The effective tax rate in the year 2010-11 is 33.99 per cent.The share of corporation tax in total tax revenue has come down from 11.56 per cent in 1970-71 to 9.27 per cent in 1990-91 as against 18.19 per cent in 1998-99.

Companies are given some tax incentives in taxationin it the depreciation compensation is mainly considered to be depreciation on any machinery, equipment, cost of houses, new plant, equipment etc. for setting up or operating companies.And other concessions are also offered.Such additional tax incentives have led to the collapse of the tax base and the emergence of many zero tax companies.Therefore, a new minimum alternative tax law has been enacted to address this problem.The taxable amount calculated by the company under this tax is less than 30% from the following year and its book profit.

The taxable amount calculated by the company under this tax is less than 30% from the following year and its book profit.The minimum alternative tax is 10 per cent of the book profit in 2007-08 and 2008-09 under Income Tax Act 115.Looking at the figures in the budget, it is clear that the corporation tax revenue has been steadily increasing from 1979-80 to 2020-21.The highest percentage change was in the year 1991-92. The percentage change is 47.20 percent and the lowest change in the corporation tax is in the year 1980-81 which is -1.10.The year 1991 initiative i.e. before the economic reforms saw a change in the corporation tax from negative to positive and then to a lesser extent.Percentage change in corporation tax in post-1991 economic reforms after liberalization, privatization and globalization this change is more or less the same as in other years.

Corporation tax revenue was Rs 1392 crore in 1979-80 and Rs 7853 crore in 1991-92.That is, the graph shows a horizontal increase in parallel growth as well as an increase in the corporation tax for the right side.Similarly, the growth of corporation tax in total tax revenue is well seen.The highest contribution of corporation tax in total tax revenue was in the year 2009-10 and the lowest contribution was in the year 1987-88.The contribution of corporation tax to the total tax revenue has been steadily increasing since 1991-92.The contribution of corporation tax in the year 2009-10 was 39.19 per cent.If you look at the graph, the growth of corporation tax in the year 1979-80 is seen to be parallel to the horizontal, parallel to this.This means that the contribution of corporation tax to total tax revenue is seen to stabilize after a few years.

In addition, the contribution of corporation tax to the total income has been increasing. In the year 1979-80, the contribution of corporation tax to the total income has been 9.03 percent.It declined to 7.51 per cent in 1991-92.Then it grew.In the year 2018-19, the contribution of corporation tax to the total revenue increased to 30.18 per cent.The contribution of corporation tax to the total revenue has been increasing since 1999-2000.If we look at the state-wise statistics, from the year 2002-03, the collection per corporation tax is seen as separate revenue.His initiative was included in his total income.The highest corporation tax paying state is Uttar Pradesh and the lowest corporation tax paying state is Goa.In Uttar Pradesh, the percentage of corporation tax in the year 2011-12 is 187.73 per cent and the percentage of corporation tax in the year 2020-21 is 432.52 per cent.The lowest corporation tax paying state in 2011-12 is Sikkim with a percentage of 2.28 per cent and the lowest corporation tax paying state in Goa in 2020-21 is 9.31 per cent.Uttar Pradesh is followed by Bihar which pays corporation tax with 104.05 per cent in 2011-12 and 242.68 per cent in 2020-21.The contribution of corporation tax to total tax has also been increasing.The Central Government levies Corporation Tax, Income Tax, Capital Gains Tax, Expenditure Tax, Customs, Excise Duty, Estate Duty, Property Tax, Bounty Tax, Service Tax on Central Area and Tax on Goods and Services.

Excise duty was Rs 14,470 crore and customs was Rs 11,475 crore in 1986-87.While corporation tax revenue was Rs 3,160 crore and income tax was Rs 2,879 crore, estate duty was Rs 14 crore, bounty tax was Rs 9 crore and property tax was Rs 174 crore.The highest revenue is from excise duty, followed by customs revenue and corporation tax revenue.Similarly, the highest revenue from central excise duty in 1991-92 after 1991 was Rs 28,110 crore and corporation tax revenue was Rs 7,853 crore.While income tax was Rs 673 crore. Capital gain tax 305Crore, property tax was Rs 307 crore, as well as bounty tax was Rs 8 crore and estate duty was Rs 3 crore and tax on central area was Rs 1265 crore while service tax was zero.The highest tax revenue of all taxes in the year 2020-21 is corporation tax which is Rs 681000 crore.It is followed by income tax at Rs 638,000 crore and customs duty at Rs 138,000 crore. And property tax is zero.Excise duty revenue is Rs 267,000 crore and goods and services tax is Rs 690,500 crore and service tax is Rs 1,020 crore.The tax on the central area is Rs 7500 crore.

Thus, in the study of corporation tax analysis, the collection of corporation tax has increased in years, but the state-wise distribution of corporation tax has been found to be uneven.For example, in Uttar Pradesh, the proportion of education, infrastructure, industries, etc. is not high, but their share in the corporation tax is the highest.The government should make efforts to ensure that equal share of corporation tax is levied in each state.In the year 2020-21, the highest corporation tax has been collected. In the year 2011-12, Gujarat ranks sixth in tax payment in India but Gujarat ranks first in growth.As on December 17, 2011, the budget tax collection in Gujarat is Rs.14821 crore which is 27.5% more than last year.Corporate tax collection in Gujarat is 81.96 percent.In which the contribution of many famous companies of Gujarat is important.

Thus, in the study of corporation tax, there have been several studies in which corporate tax has gained a very significant place as compared to other taxes.Corporate tax rates have been very high in GDP growth.The corporate world is likely to move forward in the future and its revenue will continue to increase as many corporate companies have come to India which has made India a sufficient market for the corporate world.This has created innumerable opportunities for development. If the government intervenes in it, a developing country like India can be put ahead in the competition of the world economy.

References

1. Ambirajan S.(1964), "The Taxation of Corporate Income In India" , Asia Publishing House.pp 58, 76-79.

2. Jain Indu (2003), " Taxation of Income: an international comparison,Delhi.New century publication

3. Kantadhya B.S.(2000), "Structure and reform of Taxation in India.Deep& Deep publications pvt.ltd pp.45-59

4. Trivedi Hasmukhray (1966), " CorporateIncometax, Governemnt Finance economic Analysis,GujaratUniversity,Ahd

5. Bhatt Mahesh (1992), " Principles of Public Finanace,CompanyTaxes,UniversityGranthNirmanBoard,Ahd

6. Centre for Monitoring Indian Economy (2005)

7. Report of India Tax Foundation,TaxReforms,New Delhi

8. Sandesh Newspapaer

9. www.cek.ef.uni.ij.silmagister/pandey 7-b-06 pdf

10. www.budgetindia.com

11.	http://www.docstoc.com/docs/6/69.3697/corporation tax

Dr.BHAVNA H.PARMAR has been completed M.A.,M.Phil.,(Economics)   from Gujarat University,Ahmedabad.She awarded Ph.D.from Gujarat VidhyapithAhmedabad.She has passed CCC from Dr.Ambedkar Open University Ahmedabad and computer course from AMA.She awarded Rajiv Gandhi National Feloowship for M.Phil.She has presented Research Paper of many seminar and conference and participated also.

www.ingramcontent.com/pod-product-compliance
Lightning Source LLC
LaVergne TN
LVHW041434170726
843492LV00008B/2595